MAN AND WOMAN IN CHRISTIAN PERSPECTIVE

Werner Neuer

translated by Gordon J. Wenham

Hodder & Stoughton
LONDON SYDNEY AUCKLAND TORONTO

Originally published as *Mann und Frau in Christlicher Sicht*, Giessen and Basle, Brunnen Verlag, fourth edition, 1988.

British Library Cataloguing in Publication Data
Neuer, Werner
  Man and woman in Christian perspective
  1. Sex roles – Christian viewpoints
  I. Title
  261.8'357

ISBN 0-340-51721 2

Published by Hodder and Stoughton,
a division of Hodder and Stoughton Ltd,
Mill Road, Dunton Green, Sevenoaks, Kent TN13 2YA.
Editorial Office: 47 Bedford Square, London WC1B 3DP.

Typeset by Hewer Text Composition Services, Edinburgh.
Printed in Great Britain by Richard Clay Ltd., Bungay, Suffolk.

To my wife

Contents

Translator's Preface

Sexuality is a topic many Christians are reticent about. We are all acutely conscious of our failings and prejudices in this area, and we do not want to hurt our friends who may hold quite different opinions. So most of the time we smile sweetly and keep our thoughts to ourselves.

But to avoid discussing such an important area of life is misguided, for their sex is the most vital ingredient of everyone's personality. Our first question when a baby is born is: 'Is it a boy or a girl?' And so it continues throughout life. How we view and act towards everyone we meet is to a greater or lesser extent affected by their sex. But is this right? Should parents treat their sons and daughters differently, and have different expectations for them? Is a husband's duty different from a wife's, or a mother's responsibility different from a father's? Should someone's sex be a consideration in church leadership? How far are our reactions culturally conditioned, the product of environment and upbringing? How far are our attitudes the result of prejudice? How far do they correspond to reality? May they even sometimes be God-given instincts implanted in us by our creator?

These very fundamental questions deserve serious informed discussion from a biblical and Christian perspective. This book, I believe, should help to promote such a discussion. It was first recommended to me by a German New Testament scholar. For my part, when I read it I was impressed that a systematic theologian like Werner Neuer should have such a command of the Old Testament material, which is my field, and be so skilled in the exegesis of the relevant biblical texts. Anyone therefore looking for a compact, readable, yet scholarly, treatment of the biblical texts relating to sexuality can hardly find a surer guide than Dr Neuer.

I should like to thank Dr Neuer and David Mackinder, my copy-editor, for improving my translation, Roger Beckwith for updating the material on modern liturgy, and Margaret Hardy for typing it all.

Gordon Wenham

Introduction

The place of Man and Woman in society is one of the most disputed questions of our age. More and more people are becoming convinced that the traditional ideas about the sexes must be completely revised. The view, barely contested for thousands of years, that men and women are fundamentally different in nature and therefore have different tasks in life, often prompts vigorous opposition.

Despite the witness of Holy Scripture this protest against traditional ideas has not stopped and has for a long time attracted Christians. Many regard the biblical view of man and woman as culturally conditioned and out of date. So it is no longer recognised as a binding norm for the life of believers. Even Christians who take seriously the authority of the Bible often have difficulties with accepting or just understanding the biblical view of the sexes.

In the light of this situation it is high time for Christians to consider completely afresh the biblical view of male and female and to attempt by paying careful attention to Scripture to discover what is God's will for man and woman in the present. This is the purpose of the present study. We shall try to make intelligible those biblical texts dealing with the position of the sexes which are frequently misunderstood. Though our presentation aims to be popular, it is based on thorough scholarship. We shall seek to clarify the real content of these texts and their continuing validity. We shall also present what the human and social sciences know about gender differences and analyse the issues raised by feminists both inside and outside the church. This should help the reader to survive in the modern debate about man and woman and to make the Christian view credible.

This study is not an academic theological investigation. That would require much more space and depth. Rather the book offers an intelligible yet theologically based guide for a wider circle of Christians. However, despite my endeavour to present as wide a variety of viewpoints as possible, many of necessity have been left out or just mentioned in passing. This is especially so when it comes to the practical and ethical consequences of the Christian view of man and woman, which are barely sketched in the present study. Here the book needs supplementing not just with literature, but by further reflection by all seeking God's will for men and women, whether in their own personal life or in the life of the church.

I anticipate that my ideas will meet opposition, for they contradict the way many Christians live and what they teach. I therefore urge the reader to test whatever he objects to in the light of Holy Scripture. The issues discussed here are of great moment for the life of Christ's church and the life of every individual Christian. For they concern how the will of God may be fulfilled in one of the most significant areas of human society. If this book helps us to take God and his loving will for male and female with total seriousness once again, it will have achieved its purpose.

I dedicate this book in gratitude to my life companion without whose encouragement and lively discussions it would never have been written. I should also like to thank Professor Harald Riesenfeld of Uppsala and my friends Dr Rainer Riesner, the Rev. Dietrich Sprenger and his wife Ulrike, for reading the manuscript.

Werner Neuer
Gomaringen, Advent 1980

Addition to Author's Introduction
for English Edition

It is a real joy to me that my study on the Christian understanding of man and woman is now available in English. When I sent my manuscript to the press in 1980, I never guessed that within nine years it would go through four German printings and one English. And the many complimentary comments in the form of reviews and letters that I have received from people of various denominations have far exceeded my expectations.

The present English edition, apart from a few corrections, corresponds to the second German edition. I have seen no need for greater changes of content. In fact since 1980 three large works have appeared which have substantially confirmed my position. Stephen W. Clark's *Man and Woman in Christ* (1980) confirms the abiding validity of the biblical ordering of the sexes through an abundance of biblical and sociological observation. Then in 1982 the Catholic theologian Manfred Hauke published *Women in the Priesthood?* (English translation 1988), which to my knowledge is the most thorough study of the Christian understanding of the sexes. Hauke's work deals with nearly all the relevant aspects of the subject. It covers Scripture, church history, theology, the social sciences, the study of religion, and philosophy, thus making it the most comprehensive reply to feminist theology so far published from a biblical perspective. Finally two years later the traditional biblical view of the sexes received a surprisingly empirical confirmation from Wigand Siebel's sociological investigation *Herrschaft und Liebe* (1984).

Siebel's argument is based almost entirely on sociology and does not develop the biblical perspective. But all three books offer an impressive confirmation and elaboration of the position taken in my book and can be heartily recommended to all readers prompted by my work to take the study of this topic further.

Finally, I should like to express my heartfelt gratitude to Gordon Wenham, who alongside his other duties has selflessly undertaken the translation. May the triune God bless him and all readers of this book!

Werner Neuer,
Gomaringen, September 1989

1
The Relevance of the Topic

1 The Challenge of Feminism

The nature and role of men and women are among the oldest of issues, yet they are always topical. It is therefore no surprise that the New Testament pays close attention to the relationship of man and woman and handles it showing remarkable awareness of the principles at stake. The issue of the Christian attitude to male and female is as old as Christianity itself. However, it must be said that the issue has become particularly acute in our century, since the biblically determined relationship between the sexes and with it the traditional forms of association of men and women have been radically questioned in a way never known before in history.

This questioning is most clearly seen in the feminist movement. This has been concerned since the 1960s, and particularly in the 1970s, to eliminate completely those forms of real or supposed oppression of women which still survive in social and private life, and thereby to make possible the complete emancipation of women. But also outside the feminist movement in the narrow sense may be heard loud and growing criticism of the traditional relationship of the sexes. The current feminist movement stands in a long tradition of women's movements which have existed in Europe since the last century and whose origins may be traced back to the eighteenth century.[1] But modern feminism cannot be viewed simply as the current form of the women's movements which date from the beginnings of this century.

Whereas the women's movements before the First World War were interested primarily in the political and legal equality of women (votes for women, the right to education and a career) and with that upheld, at least in Germany, relatively conservative attitudes to the character and role of the sexes, the current feminist movement is more or less intent on totally destroying the traditional conception of what constitutes male and female.

In what follows we hope to sketch as briefly as possible the fundamental convictions and aims of current feminists, without trying to give a more precise analysis of a far-from-unified stream of ideas. Such a survey is necessary for our study because certain basic attitudes of the feminist movement are also supported by those outside it; and these basic convictions are increasingly influencing our society.

The most important single forerunner of modern feminism is Simone de Beauvoir, whose book *The Second Sex* has fundamental significance for the women's movement. Simone de Beauvoir, who lived for decades with the existentialist philosopher Jean-Paul Sartre without marrying him, contests every type of naturally given difference between male and female. The historically accepted differences between the sexes, according to her, rest solely and entirely on social conditions which permit the subjugation of women by men. She sums up her thesis in the pregnant phrase, 'One is not born, but rather becomes, a woman.'[2] She thereby dispatches the question that has recurred for millennia about the givenness of sexual differences. She propagates an ideal of humanity's future beyond male and female.[3] Instead of the natural procreation of children she advocates artificial insemination.[4] She emphatically calls for the legalisation of abortion and regards its legal prohibition as absurd.[5]

Behind all this lies the idea that a woman should be completely free from the allegedly natural limits, in which according to traditional understanding she ought to live. Simone de Beauvoir's concept is based on the notion that human beings can and should determine their lives free from natural limitations. Man is not determined by his natural endowments, but by what he makes of himself.

It is not difficult to see that Simone de Beauvoir's book is more than a plea for the elimination of all political, legal and social disadvantages for women. What she is propagating is much more a cultural revolution of the most radical sort imaginable. It is a cultural revolution which puts in question all the convictions, traditions, and customs, on interactions between the sexes that have developed in the course of human history. This thrust towards a cultural revolution, and not just politico-legal demands, has been taken up and developed by the newer feminist movement.

One of the most radical publications of feminism is Shulamit Firestone's *The Dialectic of Sex: The Case for Feminist Revolution*. The book advocates the destruction of the sexist society, the complete sweeping away of gender differences.[6] Like de Beauvoir the author demands artificial procreation.[7] She wants to break up the family and to substitute the upbringing of children by groups instead of by parents.[8] Firestone's book, despite some differences from de Beauvoir's vision, fits in completely with the cultural–revolutionary direction of women's emancipation. It contains within it a revolutionising of the biological givenness of male and female: 'Feminists have to question not just all of *Western* culture, but the organization of culture itself, and further, even the very organization of nature.'[9] The feminist goal comprises, according to Firestone, much more than merely political reorientation: 'If there were another word more all-embracing than *revolution*, we would use it.'[10] In Germany Alice Schwarzer, with her book *The Little Difference* (140,000 copies) and the founding of the women's magazine *Emma*, has become for a good while the most well-known representative of German feminism. She also does not criticise just the legal and political forms of real or supposed oppression of women, but she sees in the normally accepted sexual union of men with women a means of oppression. In her view 'nothing in sexual intercourse makes it desirable for women, but much does for men'.[11] She pleads instead, as do many representatives of feminism, for homosexual activity by women. So too Alice Schwarzer couples the idea of emancipation with an attack on the foundations of human existence given by nature.

It would take us too far afield to examine in greater detail the plans of Simone de Beauvoir and Shulamit Firestone or the convictions of Alice Schwarzer. A review of feminist literature, now too vast to survey, is also neither possible nor necessary. It only needs to be shown how radically all received ideas about maleness and femaleness are being questioned today. There is in feminism the tendency either to deny completely, or to count as insignificant, all sexual differences apart from the incontestably biological ones. The non-biological differences between men and women are *socially* conditioned and therefore seen as open to correction.[12]

This outlook obviously stands in complete contrast to the conviction hitherto dominant in human history that the sexes are by nature fundamentally different. True, what the difference consisted of was differently understood in different periods and cultures. That there is such a difference of nature was undisputed.[13] Universal convictions and patterns of behaviour can be established which express the fundamental differentiation of the sexes, and these are found in all cultures studied so far.[14]

This fact is naturally no disproof of feminism. It shows in the first place only how unusual and novel are modern feminist convictions. Hitherto feminism has had relatively few supporters, but it is now no longer a fringe movement with negligible influence. For one thing the number of its sympathisers is very large, and for another feminism is still a young and growing movement. Just the last decade has seen a flood of women's literature, journals, and shops inside and outside Germany. Action against the prohibition of abortion and also protest against rape have met with considerable support. Feminism is an unmistakable sign of the worldwide uncertainty about the nature and role of the sexes. For this reason it poses a challenge to every responsible person and also to the Christian.

2 The Church and Feminism

In the church and in theology too a 'feminism' has grown up
which portrays the emancipation of women as a demand of
the gospel.[15] This demand, it is said, has been given an
inadequate place in the church and in theology. This has led
to a church dominated by men and by one-sidedly masculine
ways of thought. Church feminism is therefore working for
the maximum possible influence of women in church leadership and a revision of male-shaped theology. Admission of
women to the pastorate or priesthood is a fundamental
demand. Exclusion of women from the pastorate is seen
as discriminatory and contradicting the gospel. Feminist
theology is concerned with a new orientation in exegesis to
bring out the Bible's positive evaluation of women[16] and in
dogmatics with the revision of the traditional concept of God.
The received picture of God as father must be completed
through a picture of God as mother.[17] Thus feminist theology
is intent on a feminist piety, which prays to God both as father
and mother.

Theological feminism leads also to a new kind of biblical
criticism. All biblical passages which express the subordination of women to men are rejected as historically conditioned,
in favour of those passages which express the full equality of
the sexes. The aim is the so-called 'non-sexist use'[18] of
Scripture, free of any form of discrimination against women.
Feminist theology claims to be based on Jesus himself. Hence
the provocative title of an American essay: 'Jesus was a
Feminist.'[19]

This glance at the character and goals of feminist theology
must suffice for introduction, for in this study we must time
and again interact with it. Just as with feminism outside the
church, so this theological feminism is something brand new.
Should it establish itself, it would revolutionise Christian
theology, the church, and piety, as it stands in sharp contrast
to earlier tradition, however much disagreement there is
among feminists on individual points.

Feminist theology arose in the USA, and it can now boast

an impressive number of publications. The National Council of Churches (NCC), to which thirty-two Protestant and Orthodox churches belong, has produced a revised translation of the Bible, used in the 'Inclusive Language Lectionary', in which male descriptions of God and male pronouns are reduced to a minimum to eliminate the alleged sexism in the Bible. 'Abba, Father' becomes 'God, my Mother and Father'. In the 1979 American Episcopal Prayer Book and the 1985 Canadian Book of Alternative Services, a lectionary is adopted in which all references to female subordination in the congregation and other unfashionable ideas are cut out, even in the continuous reading of the New Testament in the daily readings. The New Zealand Prayer Book follows suit and goes even further, speaking of 'God as Father' rather than 'God the Father', a mode rather than a person. These examples show that feminist theology already has considerable influence in many parts of the English-speaking world. In Germany, however, theological feminism is not so far advanced, but is gaining ever more influence. In February 1979 the first German conference on feminist theology took place in Bad Boll,[20] and since then this theology has enjoyed increasing influence and publicity. Church feminism (like secular feminism) is a very diverse movement. It may be combined with quite conservative theology (*e.g.*, the evangelical 'Biblical Feminists' in the USA), but it can also adopt explicitly extreme tendencies.[21] Church feminism is part of the general feminist movement, but the two should be clearly distinguished. Compared with secular feminism, church feminism tends to be more moderate and it basically accepts both theology and the church.

Theological feminism presents a challenge to both theology and the church, for it poses questions which affect the substance of two thousand years of Christian tradition. It continues in an even sharper and more fundamental form the discussion which has taken place in the Protestant churches during the last twenty years in connection with the ordination of women to the pastoral ministry. This has already posed the question how far the biblical ordering of the sexes is still valid for Christians today. This question was topical long before feminist theology arose, and it is still topical today for those Christians who reject feminist theology for biblical reasons.

3 The Necessity for a Christian Response

The first two sections have shown how urgently a Christian response to the question of the nature and role of the sexes is needed. Christians must take up the challenge for God's sake and for humanity's sake. For God's sake, because they are commissioned to recognise God's will for male and female and to put it into practice. For humanity's sake, because their uncertain contemporaries are thirsting for directions on the basic questions of life. When God's will for the fundamental relationship of male and female remains unobserved, there are the gravest consequences for human life and conduct, even if God is obeyed in other spheres. The Christian view of the sexes must be founded on the will of God for men and women; it cannot grow out of arbitrary reflection. This means that the Christian view of male and female must arise from the Bible as the valid norm of Christian theology. For this reason the heart of this book is what Holy Scripture has to say about the relationship of male and female (see Chapters 5–8). Since the Bible also contains remarks that are directed at particular situations or that are historically conditioned, biblical statements about male and female must be tested to see how far they are still valid today (see Chapter 10).

A Christian view of the sexes is supported not only by considering the decisive biblical texts but by drawing on experimental knowledge about male and female. This is the more necessary in our discussion, because, apart from bodily differences, feminism disputes the differentiation of the sexes. We shall therefore bring into our study the differences between male and female that have been established by scientific investigation (see Chapter 4).

This study addresses a multitude of questions and attitudes.

It must therefore be explicitly emphasised that despite the variety of aspects considered the focus of our study is the theological view of male and female. The following discussion is not to be understood primarily as a response to the questions of feminism, but as a response to the question, What is God's will for the sexes in the present situation? The decisive question for the Christian is never whether he can supply a satisfactory answer to the ideological queries of his time but whether he is obedient to the will of God for his time. In every respect the Christian is freed from bondage to the spirit of the age and is bound only to obey God. The Christian theologian, in expounding the biblical view of man and woman, is in no way required to give an explicit answer to all the questions thrown up by feminism. Rather it suffices to make clear *God's* role for the sexes in an intelligible and contemporary way.

This study would like to contribute to the clarification of the biblical teaching on this issue. The deeper the insight Christians have into *God's* aims and intentions, the more aptly and relevantly they can answer mankind's questions and expose the perversity of human aims. In so far as our study serves to clarify God's will for man and woman, it will also indirectly serve the Christian debate with feminism inside and outside the church.

2

The Distinction Between the Equality and the Identity of the Sexes

In this chapter we aim to clarify two important terms in the discussion, equality and identity. Too often it is argued that if the sexes are equal, they must also be identical and do the same things. In the personal realm equality signifies that people have the same dignity and value; it does not necessarily imply that they are the same in nature or do the same sort of jobs. For the latter concept we prefer to use the word identity.

The distinction between the equality and identity of the sexes is a basic presupposition of the Christian view of male and female. Without this distinction the Christian view cannot be understood. In studying the biblical texts we shall constantly come across this distinction, even when it is not mentioned in so many words. Even outside the Bible equality and identity must be carefully distinguished for the sake of clarity. The failure to make such a distinction in discussing the nature and functions of the sexes has already been disastrous and leads to serious error. It is therefore necessary to point out that the equality of the sexes in no way entails their identity. Conversely the differences between men and women do not at all call in question their equality.

The Christian view of the sexes starts from the premise that both men and women are in every respect God's creatures and of equal value, but that in their being they are fundamentally distinct. Consequently they have different tasks to fulfil. In our section on the biblical teaching we shall establish and elucidate this more clearly (see Chapters 5–8).

The intrinsic differentiation of men and women means that the sexes are not only physiologically different, but also psychologically. The assumption that sexual differences include body, soul, and spirit is an essential part of a Christian view of men and women, but it is by no means a specifically Christian conviction. We shall see in Chapters 3 and 4 that this assumption is independent of religion or philosophy and rests on experience and scientific observation.

The presupposition of the equality of men and women is also not specifically a Christian one. It is found associated with all sorts of religious and philosophical viewpoints. However, it must be said that the wide acceptance today that the sexes are equal is largely to be ascribed to Christianity. Ultimately too this assumption is adequately based only on faith in a personal creator.[22]

The assumption of the equality of men and women is at least in the Christian world taken for granted. This must not blind us to the fact that the conviction that women were of less value was stubbornly maintained into the twentieth century. The intellectual history of Europe, from the Greeks down to Kant, Nietzsche and Schopenhauer, is full of misogynist remarks.[23] As late as 1908 the book *On the Physiological Weakness of Women* by the doctor P. J. Möbius went into its ninth edition.[24] The saddest product of misogynist attitudes in our century must be the work of the Kantian philosopher, O. Weininger, whose book *Sex and Character* was reprinted twenty-five times in ten years. In it women are not simply stated to be of less worth intellectually and morally, but worthless, indeed evil.[25] The wide circulation of such books as those by Möbius and Weininger means they cannot be dismissed simply as the utterances of crazy individuals. They must be seen as evidence of a widespread conviction that women are less valuable, a conviction which happily has waned in the intellectual climate of the latter half of this century, so that such publications are no longer taken seriously. That is not to say, though, that the devaluation of women no longer consciously or subconsciously influences contemporary thought. For it is certain that the devaluation of women *in practice* is still widespread today. One only needs to mention the subjugation of wives to despotic husbands in many marriages, the degradation of women as sex objects in many films, magazines, in advertising, literature and pornography and in the shocking number of sexual assaults.

By distinguishing between the equality and the identity of the sexes we have already found one criterion for evaluating the truth and error in feminism. Feminism tends to confuse the real equality of men and women with their being identical, something which is contrary to the facts.[26] The feminist movement is right to campaign against every theoretical and practical devaluation of women in the private, social, and political realms. In so far as feminism does this on an ethical basis, it can only be applauded. However, feminism is wrong to reject a specifically gender-based distribution of male and female functions. Behind this rejection lies a fundamentally wrong view of the sexes, which inevitably leads feminism to unrealistic and therefore destructive consequences. A Christian view of male and female must support the true insights of feminism and correct its false presuppositions in order to make possible the genuine liberation of men and women to fulfil their divinely created destiny.

3

Sexual Differences and the Integrity of the Personality

Having tried to define the difference between the terms identity and equality, we must once again attempt to clarify very briefly some of the basic concepts involved in discussing sexual differences. It is our conviction that both Scripture and experience show that man is an integral unity, and that this has profound implications for understanding human personality and particularly for the place of sexuality within the human constitution. In this chapter it is our aim to spell out some of the main implications of this view of human nature. We are not at this stage trying to prove them, simply to sketch a framework for the later more detailed discussion.

While happily the equality of the sexes is widely accepted today, even if often denied in practice, the nature of the differences between the sexes is widely contested. That men and women are physiologically different is so obvious that it needs no further discussion. That they are also psychologically fundamentally different is doubted not only by radical feminists but by many other contemporaries. It is questioned whether there is a recognisable male nature or female nature which determines the whole of life and character. Sexuality is understood to be a purely physiological aspect of humanity that has no relationship to the psychological life.

This idea proves to be untenable on further examination, for it conflicts with the integrity of human personality. A person is a total unity of body and soul[27] which cannot be split into a sexual corpse and a sexless psyche.[28] This indivisible unity of the inner and outer life, of soul and body, is a fact which is daily experienced, is demonstrated by science,[29] and is borne witness to by the Bible.[30]

Body and soul stand in a very close relationship to each other and mutually influence each other. Since soul and body form an inseparable unity, being male or female characterises the whole person and not only his or her body. The Catholic philosopher and theologian Fritz Leist correctly observes: 'Sexuality is not simply something bodily or physiological . . . The body is the great and comprehensive sign, in which the being and nature of the person is expressed.'[31]

A person exists only as a man or as a woman. A person can never deny his maleness or her femaleness. A person does not just have a male or female body, he is a man or she is a woman. Sex is therefore not just one personal characteristic among others, but a mode of being which determines one's whole life. 'Sexuality is the ultimate, irremoveable and irreplaceable mode, which makes a person the kind of person he or she is.'[32]

It is therefore incorrect to separate a person's being from their sexuality and to view the person as an essentially sexless intellect to which their sex is attached, not as part of their being, but as something external that is only important for the propagation of the species. E. Metzke has justly pointed out that all Western philosophy tends to the view that 'the true being of a person has nothing to do with sexual differences'.[33] This attitude still has great influence. In the past it often led to devaluing sexuality as merely animal. Sexuality hindered a person's real intellectual destiny and therefore was accepted only as a necessary evil or else rejected entirely. The history of Christendom is not free from such tendencies.[34] It is of vital importance in approaching human sexuality to regard it as an essential mark of the person, something that determines the whole being. For then it is no longer possible to view sexual activity as in opposition to a supposedly sexless intellectual–spiritual life and therefore of less worth.

How far sexuality involves the intellectual and spiritual realm is beautifully illustrated in the attraction between the sexes. In every healthy loving relationship between man and woman the attraction of one for the other rests not merely on the sexual drive but on the erotic fascination caused by the intellectual and spiritual differences in the lovers. The lover desires the other as a total person. He wants a complete communion not only physically, but also mentally and spiritually. It is a hallmark of true love to desire the person of the beloved and not just their body. Love between a man and a woman is thus a good example of how sexuality involves the whole person.

Since the whole person is governed by one's sex, physiological differences between the sexes correspond to psychological differences. The following example illustrates very clearly the correspondence of sex-determined physiological and sex-determined psychological differences: a woman's skin is demonstrably more sensitive than a man's.[35] She is therefore more open to pleasant sensations aroused by touch. This greater tactile sensitivity matches a greater psychological sensitivity, a deeper empathy for other people and their needs.[36] This one example must suffice for the moment to illustrate how physiology and psychology match up with sexuality. In the next chapter we shall explore these connections more precisely.

We can therefore conclude that sexuality involves the whole person and constitutes part of one's essential being. Sexual differences affect not only the bodily aspects, but also the psychological aspects of personality. Body and soul form a unity which cannot be divided into a sexual part (body) and a sexless part (mind). Rather the person in its totality is a sexual being.

The understanding of human sexuality as a totality which is sketched here stands in sharp contrast to the popular understanding of it in terms of roles. This interprets the usual gender-specific modes of behaviour merely as roles which society allocates to men and women. We shall try in an excursus to show that this role theory model is questionable.

Excursus 1
Role theory: does it deal adequately with the male/female relationship?

Popular modern role theory[37] starts from the premise that everyone has a collection of roles to play in order to fulfil the usual roles expected of them by society. So, for example, a man must play the role of husband, father, teacher, consumer and citizen. For each of these roles society has certain expectations which a person must play out if he or she does not want to clash with the traditions and goals of society. Education has the task of equipping people to accept these roles and thereby to become social beings. In all areas of life people are forced to assume certain roles. The Lutheran adult catechism even describes being a Christian as a role: 'My role as a Christian, as partner of God.'[38]

Role theory as briefly sketched here began in sociology, and since then has exercised significant influence on educational theory and practice in Germany. The real trademark of role theory is its understanding of man to be a *product of the society*; and it is society which gives him various expected roles to play. It would take us too far afield to distinguish more precisely the truth and error in role theory. The sociologist R. Dahrendorf has done this in a remarkable way in his book *Homo Sociologicus*.[39] For our investigation the only important question is whether it is actually justifiable to speak of the roles of man, woman, father, and mother.

The concept of role is a theatrical concept and denotes the part given to an actor. The role given to an actor is usually something foreign to him with which he identifies only in the play. In a role he does not portray himself, but someone else. And even when he in broad measure internally identifies with the role and uses it to portray himself (which is often the case), the role portrayed remains only a play which does not directly express the actual thought and will of the actor.

We have determined already that sexuality is not just something important but extrinsic to one's nature, but that it belongs rather to the very essence of a person and determines their whole conduct. If that is really so, then the inappropriateness of role theory for understanding sexuality is obvious. A person does not play the role of a man or a woman, but he is a man or she is a woman. Sex is no role, that can be changed at will like stage roles, but is a fundamental aspect of human existence from which no one can escape. It carries with it quite definite tasks and modes of conduct. And language must reflect this state of affairs. It is therefore sensible to speak of 'being a man', 'being a woman' or 'being a father' or 'being a mother', of 'masculinity, femininity, fatherhood or motherhood' and of the tasks that flow from these states. This terminology makes it clear that sex is concerned with being and not with roles that are played at the dictate of external constraints such as society. The concept of sexual roles is meaningful, though, in the case of homosexuality, where men play the role of women and women play the role of men. The very fact that the concept of role fits perverted sexual behaviour shows how unsuitable it is to describe the natural created relationships of men and women.

In the cause of truth we should therefore give up talking about the roles of the sexes, for it obscures the essential sexuality of people. It also gives a false impression that observable differences in behaviour and the different distribution of tasks between the sexes are merely the product of society and may therefore be corrected by society. It must certainly be admitted – and here the concept of roles does have some validity – that society does have a significant influence on the conduct of the sexes. But what is decisive is that society can only influence positively or negatively the male or female nature which already exists, and this influence is limited by natural capacities, some of which constitute boundaries which cannot be crossed. In a later chapter we shall show that the sexually specific modes of male and female behaviour are primarily determined by bodily structure and only secondarily by society.

Role theory is a one-sided sociological theory which overemphasises the significance of society and fails to recognise the significance of created reality. It is a typical product of the overemphasis on the human contribution to history at the expense of nature, which places limits on human existence. Behind this overemphasis on history, most obvious in Marxism, lies an overemphasis on human creativity and an underemphasis on the limitations placed on man by God through nature.

4

The Differences Between Male and Female

Preliminary Observations

Every description of the differences between the sexes brings with it a hidden danger, namely that sexual differentiation is so emphasised that what male and female have in common is forgotten. So before we turn to the differences between the sexes we must reaffirm that what men and women have in common is much greater than their differences. For both are *human*, even if they realise humanity differently. Being a man or a woman constitutes a different way of expressing *the humanity that both share equally*. The following remarks will be fundamentally misunderstood if this is overlooked.

Secondly, it must be appreciated that many of the differences between the sexes are statistical generalisations. The fact that the average man is taller than the average woman does not rule out a few women being taller than most men, or a few men being shorter than most women. Similarly to recognise that women are typically better linguists than men and that the female spirit is more sympathetic than the male does not prevent some men being excellent linguists or having more empathy than some women. It is important to bear these points in mind especially when exceptionally gifted individuals of either sex are mentioned. The appearance of the occasional mathematical genius among women no more disproves the general superiority of men over women in mathematics than the brilliant male linguist disproves the general inferiority of men to women when it comes to learning languages.

Our description of gender differences may appear relatively lengthy for a theological book. But in view of the widespread questioning of essential differences between the sexes it is sensible to treat the scientifically established differences between male and female more thoroughly. Our description must leave out of consideration many of the gender differences that research has discovered. The reader who is specially interested in this area should consult the specialist literature, of which there is an abundance.[40]

1   Physiological Differences Between the Sexes[41]

Quite deliberately we begin our summary of differences between men and women with a sketch of physiological gender difference, for here such differences are particularly obvious. In so doing we are not concerned merely to list bodily differences, but to ask how far physiological differences express psychological ones or the different functions of the sexes. Our procedure is justified by the recognition that the human person is a unity of body and soul (cf. Chapter 3). This means that in some way the psychological character of a person is depicted in their body.

Josef Rötzer, a doctor, put it correctly: 'When the person is viewed as a body-soul unity, it follows that the physical prefigures the psychological. If body and soul are just two aspects of one and the same being, each aspect must say something essential about the whole.'[42] Because the human body and soul constitute a unity, it follows that the intellectual life of a person is expressed through their bodily appearance. The body may therefore be understood as 'the great and comprehensive sign in which a person's essential nature is shown forth'.[43] The philosopher Franz von Baader rightly described the relationship between the body and the mental life: 'The so-called perceptible material nature is symbolic of the inner mental life.'[44] Such an understanding of the human body obviously contradicts the widely held modern view that the human body is no more than that of a highly developed mammal.[45] Such a view misses the fact that the unique spiritual nature of man which sets him fundamentally apart from the animal world finds expression in the human body, so that despite many similarities the human body is characteristically different from all other mammals. One of many examples which could be cited is the human larynx, to which there is no parallel in the animal world. Only the human larynx is capable of speech, thereby enabling a man's spirit to be revealed and to communicate.[46] We see then that a person's body is the expression and tool of his spirit: the body allows the soul to become active and to develop. The psychologist Philip Lersch expressed the situation aptly: 'The body is the organ of life. In the body's activity the soul comes to expression. Or more precisely, life becomes animated experience through the soul's activity.'[47] Lersch correctly points out that because of their unity body and soul limit and interpret each other. He concludes that 'apparent bodily differences offer the most obvious and objective way of illuminating psychological gender differences'.[48] This inner relationship of physiological and psychological gender differences will be sketched in the important examples that follow.

First of all we want to compare the bone structure of the sexes. The male skeleton is usually stronger than the woman's. The bones are thicker and heavier. 'The greater strength of its bone structure obviously equips the man's body better than the woman's to overcome physical obstacles and to carry loads.'[49] The man has greater steadiness, strength, and stress resistance due to his stronger bones. The fact, for example, that the man's hand is stronger and bonier than the woman's 'points to the fact that the man is built to control the environment practically and creatively, whereas the softer daintier woman's hand is more suited to taking in hand the environment and looking after and caring for it protectively'.[50]

The bone structure differs between the sexes not only quantitatively in regard to its weight, but also qualitatively as regards its shape. A man's bones are more angular, more rugged in shape, while 'the woman's have rounder, less sharply marked forms and blunter corners'.[51] Women's bones are not 'merely finer, thinner and more graceful, but also softer, rounder and less rugged in shape'.[52] The more angular shape of the male body is more fitted for resistance, assaults and pushing than the rounder female body is.[53]

There are also characteristic differences between the sexes, not just in their bone structure but also in their muscles. The striated muscles in men are more strongly developed and constructed than women's. They serve above all for dealing with external obstacles. Wherever we manipulate, model or effect the environment, the striated muscles come into action. The man's superior equipment in this respect and his stronger bone structure indicate that by nature the male rather than the female is designed to overcome external environmental obstacles, to reshape and master the environment. The woman is also naturally active, and is particularly concerned with things in her immediate environment. But her activity does not involve her much in pushing forward and overcoming external obstacles, so much as in 'caring and nursing, in sorting, tidying and polishing'.[54] 'A woman's muscles are particularly suited to their tasks. They are by nature less suited to strong contractions than to active compliance at the right moment.[55]

This fact is intimately related to the maternal responsibility of women. Their abdomens are designed to withstand very severe strains in pregnancy. The suitability of women's muscles to their tasks matches a similar capability of women in the psychological realm. 'The woman's psyche, just like her muscles, can adapt very rapidly to every internal and external change. The average woman adjusts mentally and physiologically to external circumstances with versatility and adaptability.'[56] The relative lack of muscle in women, which incidentally is not culturally conditioned but is the result of hormonal differences,[57] is compensated for by more fat. As a result of this, and the shape of the bones already mentioned, the woman's body is rounder and the man's more angular.[58]

We may sum up by saying that the man's bodily frame is fitted for remoulding the environment, 'while the woman's bodily shape expresses her greater gifts in arranging and caring for a circumscribed world of the nearest and most intimate things'.[59]

The woman's skin is much softer, more tender, and smoother than a man's. Women are therefore more aware of the pleasures of touch.[60] This greater sensitivity of the skin matches the greater sensitivity of women in the psychological realm, their ability to approach matters carefully, their greater adaptability and sympathy, their capacity to give and take and to go along with situations; whereas the man tends to try to alter reality by changing it.[61]

One of the most characteristic differences as far as the secondary sexual organs are concerned is the breast. It is not just the mother's uterus but the female breast itself that points to motherhood as the woman's destiny. The Dutch biologist Buytendijk points out that only woman, in contrast with all other highly developed animals, has the physical appearance of motherhood without being or becoming a mother.[62] This fact shows that the woman is built for motherhood as the goal and fulfilment of her being. Of course that does not mean that a woman can only find fulfilment by becoming a biological mother. For the capacity for natural motherhood matches the motherliness in a woman's psychological make-up, which may be developed even if biological motherhood is denied her.[63]

A woman's motherliness consists in her particular 'supportiveness and willingness to care',[64] for which she is especially equipped through her tremendous gift of sympathy and identification with others, and through her strong natural attraction to children. The object of motherliness is 'the child, the isolated human being . . . in so far as he is small, weak, unequipped and in need of help'.[65] The motherliness peculiar to women usually finds its scope not just in looking after her own children or those of others, but in all those who in any way need help and support. This is aptly brought out in the verse

Being mother does not mean: hugging just one's own.
Being mother also means: caring for everyone.

Research into children's games has shown how strongly women are designed for motherhood.[66] Already at a very early age one can see that playing at families is inspired and led by girls. Without a 'mother' prompting and leading there is no playing at families. Even when boys join in the 'mother' quite clearly takes the lead.[67] Whereas boys prefer to play at public life and enjoy technical games, girls prefer playing houses.[68] Girls aged just three or four playing with dolls can be observed to show a great need to care. Dolls and toy animals, 'even favourite things like spoons or rattles, will be fed, put to bed or bathed'.[69] Later we shall bring additional observations to support the centrality of motherhood in the woman's life.

Our investigation of the bodily differences between the sexes has shown in an emphatic way how far these differences between men and women highlight the psychological character, the nature and the destiny of the sexes, although so far we have only looked at the so-called secondary sexual differences. Now we shall consider the primary sexual differences (the sexual organs) and deepen our earlier insights.

The sexual organs serve the purpose of procreation and the establishment of new life. They thereby point to the man's natural function of begetting and the woman's of bearing. They also point to the man's appointment to fatherhood and the woman's to motherhood. So we shall now try to investigate the character of begetting and bearing as it is determined by the structure of the reproductive organs in the act of sexual intercourse. Then we shall look into the nature of fatherhood and motherhood, which are the consequences of reproduction.

The design of the sexual organs has as its consequence that the man as begetter in the act of intercourse is the active, giving and life-creating party, while the woman as the bearer is the passive, receiving and life-sustaining party. 'Female *passivity* and male *activity*, female *letting-it-happen* and male *effecting* it, female *receiving* and male *outpouring*, female *being found* and male *seeking and acquiring* characterise the physical interaction of sexual intercourse.'[70] While the man has the more leading role and makes the ultimate decision if and when union takes place, the behaviour of the woman is that of loving subjection, which she fulfils through the offering of her body. In sexual intercourse, then, the sexes contribute differently to reproduction, so that the man as the active and leading partner and the woman as the more passive and submissive partner fulfil physical union.

What happens immediately after sexual intercourse shows a similar polarity of male activity and female passivity: male sperms vigorously swirl around the resting female egg, until one sperm penetrates the egg and fertilises it. Beforehand 'the life, which is woken by fertilisation in the female womb, lay slumbering. Then penetrated by the male sperm, it is awoken and brought into development.'[71] The activity of the man and his sperm, and the more passive action of the woman and her egg, must not obscure the fact that both sexes contribute equally to shaping the genetically inherited characteristics of the new life. The idea widespread in antiquity and the Middle Ages and even sometimes today that the semen creates life by itself and only needs the woman as soil in which to grow and develop must be decisively rejected.

The contrast between male activity and female passivity in the act of reproduction is only a provisional and approximate characterisation of what happens in sexual intercourse. For while the man's conduct is fittingly described as active, the woman's is not quite appropriately described as passive. For in physical union she is not an inactive other, but she participates as a loving, submitting, and therefore active partner. It is therefore more exact to describe the woman's conduct as receptive. However, it is true to say that in physical union the man is more active than the woman, so that the usual contrast of activity and passivity is quite useful as an approximate simplification.

In the physical union of man and woman fundamental differences between the sexes are revealed which are also apparent in their intellectual and psychological life. The latter differences are based on the physiological differences and are apparent whether or not men and women are involved in acts of sexual intercourse.

Theodorich Kampmann has summed up this difference as *spontaneity* and *receptivity*.[72] A man's life is characterised more by spontaneity than a woman's: a woman's life is characterised more by receptivity than a man's. By spontaneity Kampmann understands productive self-initiated activity. By receptivity he understands 'the capacity to receive and take over, the capacity of emotional resonance and sympathy'.[73] In fact a multitude of observations show that Kampmann's distinction has aptly expressed one of the most fundamental sexual differences. Among examples of the man's greater spontaneity one may cite his greater drive,[74] greater aggressiveness,[75] greater desire for leadership[76] and his particular capacity for creative achievements in all fields of intellectual life,[77] a sort of 'intellectual procreative ability' analogous to his biological procreativity.

The greater receptivity of woman is seen in her greater ability and willingness to imitate,[78] her greater adaptability[79] and suggestibility,[80] her greater linguistic aptitude[81] and her superior capacity to sympathise,[82] which rests on her greater sensitivity to people's expression of feeling.

Our analysis of the physical build of the sexes also showed the greater spontaneity of men and the more pronounced receptivity of women. While a man is more strongly equipped for creative or destructive remodelling of his environment, the woman is more strongly equipped for arranging what the man has acquired for her or she has received from him.[83] We see, therefore, that male spontaneity and female receptivity, which are apparent in sexual intercourse, depict fundamental characteristics of the sexes which deeply determine their whole existence, including their intellectual and spiritual life. Since male spontaneity and female receptivity in intercourse are conditioned by their sexual organs, these point symbolically to spontaneity and receptivity as characteristics of men and women, which also characterise their lives independently of the act of sexual union.

The design of the sexual organs is not only a pointer to the real spontaneity of the man and the receptivity of the woman, but also a pointer to the man's natural destiny of fatherhood and the woman's of motherhood. A man becomes a father by begetting, a woman becomes a mother through conception and giving birth. The physical contribution of the man is thus fleeting in comparison with the bodily processes which the woman undertakes in motherhood. While a man simply becomes a father through begetting, conception is for the woman only the beginning of a period of far-reaching burdens and demands. These comprise not only the nine months of pregnancy and the often painful birth, but also the period of breast-feeding which normally follows immediately. As can be seen among primitive peoples, breast-feeding may last from two to four years,[84] and only in developed countries has it been reduced artificially to several weeks or months. Thus the directly biological aspect of motherhood is far more comprehensive than the biological aspect of fatherhood, which is simply limited to the act of procreation. This corresponds to the fact that the woman's body is far more determined by her potential motherhood than a man's is by his potential fatherhood.

Here may be mentioned not only the sexual organs, which take up much more space in a woman than in a man, and the breasts, which in contrast to the rest of the animal world make her look like a mother even if she is not one at all, but also the monthly cycle which prepares an egg every month for fertilisation. As is well known, the monthly cycle, whose purpose is motherhood, has a marked influence not just on the physical but also the psychological life of a woman.[85] Its far-reaching influence on body and soul 'cannot be understood except as an urgent hint from nature, a hint of the creator's wisdom hidden within nature. The female organism is built for procreation and conception, for carrying and giving birth to, for nourishing and bringing up of children.'[86] How much the woman's body is built for motherhood is seen in the fact that failure to become a mother increases the danger of physical illness and psychological depression.[87] We see, then, that the woman's body is much more directed towards motherhood than the man's is towards fatherhood.

To grasp the overwhelming significance of motherhood for women's life, we cannot stop here though. We must go one step further. Hitherto it has only been a question of the biological aspects of maternity (pregnancy, birth, feeding), such as may similarly be observed among other mammals. But the motherhood of women goes far beyond the primary maternal functions and may be distinguished from motherhood in the whole animal world. While the maternal role lasts only quite a short time even among the higher mammals, it comprises for women (if they have, let us say, three children) at least twenty years. The human being is, as the biologist Portmann has put it, a physiological premature birth, who requires a much more intensive and lengthier nurture and upbringing than the offspring of other animals.[88]

Human motherhood is therefore a much more comprehensive role than elsewhere in the animal kingdom. Hence it is a total falsification of the facts (particularly of the character and uniqueness of the human race) when today being a mother is reduced to a few small biological functions (pregnancy, birth and breast-feeding). Such a view overlooks the fact that an intellectual–psychological motherliness belongs to motherhood without which biological motherhood will not achieve its goal of raising children into viable people. The biological functions of motherhood among human beings are only the beginning of a lengthy caring and educative role in which the woman is compelled to unfold her mental and psychological motherliness in a comprehensive and diverse manner.

We want to conclude our sketch of the physical differences between the sexes with some comments on the comprehensiveness of sexual differentiation in the human body. The physical differences between men and women are not exhausted by the primary and secondary sexual features we have described, but they also involve the cell structure. Whereas male cells contain a Y-chromosome and an X-chromosome, female cells have two X-chromosomes.[89] 'This difference involves *all* the cells of the organism; probably the real personal differences between the sexes are determined by this.'[90] Sexuality affects the *whole* of a person's body and not only a part. It is also evident in different hormone levels,[91] in the different constitution of the blood and bodily liquids,[92] of the nervous system,[93] of internal organs[94] and brain structure.[95]

The mortality of the sexes also differs. According to Kampmann the ratio of male to female conceptions is 150 to 100, but owing to the greater mortality of male embryos the ratio of births is 106 boys to 100 girls. By the fourth year of life the surplus of boys has disappeared, and at every age more men die than women. Life expectancy in industrialised nations is years shorter for men than women. The most recent research suggests that this difference mainly depends on the woman's constitution (and is therefore inherited) and not on the different conditions of life of men and women.[96]

The physiological differences between the sexes discussed here make it sufficiently clear how much sexuality determines the whole physical existence of mankind in various ways. The totality of physiological differences between the sexes is symbolic of the totality of their intellectual and psychological differentiation, on which we shall concentrate in the next sections.

Of course our discussions of the all-embracing place of sexuality need one significant qualification. Every person possesses to a certain extent sexually specific characteristics of the other sex. This goes for biological as well as intellectual and psychological aspects. So in this way there is neither a 'total man' nor a 'total woman'.[97] This recognition should save us from upholding a concept of masculinity or femininity that is removed from reality or misunderstanding the given differences between men and women as absolute contrasts.

2 The Intellectual and Psychological Differences Between the Sexes

The preceding section on the physiological differences between men and women has already brought out a whole series of intellectual and psychological differences. Mankind's body–soul unity implies that the whole person, including his or her intellectual and psychological constitution, is determined by his or her sex. In fact numerous investigations confirm that there are noticeable intellectual and psychological differences in character between the sexes. But before we look more closely at the results of research, we must point out a possible misunderstanding. When the superiority of one sex over the other in regard to various aptitudes is repeatedly asserted, it is not meant that in some areas every man is superior to every woman and that in other areas every woman is superior to every man, but only that on average one sex is superior to the other in the relevant area. We are dealing, therefore, only with statistical judgements about differences in aptitudes between the sexes, in which exceptions in varying degrees are possible.

Let us begin with intellectual cognitive differences between the sexes. Studies lasting six years on about eighty thousand young Americans aged nine, thirteen, seventeen and twenty-six to thirty-six years noted distinctive differences in aptitude. 'In Mathematics, Science and Social Studies the women remain the weaker sex.' But they are the more musical and write better essays.[98] Up to about nine years old both the urge to learn and the level of success were about equal in boys and girls, but thereafter they showed characteristic differences. The tests disclosed a great

advantage in adult males in Mathematics, Physics and Chemistry, while women could hold their own only in Biology. Similarly men clearly outdistanced the female sex in the knowledge of economic, political, geographical and historical areas. Girls were superior in 'life' disciplines up to thirteen years old . . . in all four age groups they maintained their superiority in both the theory and practice of music.[99]

Cognitive differences between the sexes may be summed up under two major headings, which have been experimentally established by all researches carried out for half a century: the verbal superiority of women and the superiority of men in spatial conceptualisation and abstract thinking.[100] Already in boys one can establish

a superiority in those intellectual abilities which presuppose logical consistency and spatial conceptualisation. This superiority in spatial conceptualisation leads to boys' superiority in technical tasks. The difference in technical aptitude which is already detectable when schooling begins grows with time so that in adolescence boys' achievements in this area may be 50 to 100% greater than girls'.[101]

On the other hand girls show a markedly greater linguistic aptitude. 'They construct words and sentences more quickly, their articulation and fluency are better, and they seem to learn to read more easily.'[102] The difference in aptitudes between the sexes in the realm of non-linguistic (spatial-abstract) thinking is greater than in verbal capabilities, and the latter differences reduce with age.[103] The more developed spatial reasoning ability among men explains the fact that in mathematical, scientific and technical areas of research and industry many more men are to be found than women. Because of their greater linguistic aptitude more girls undertake language study. The French sociologist, Sullerot, points out that in the mechanical engineering industry the number of professional women engineers is declining, even in Eastern Europe, where there has been a strong effort to push girls in this direction.[104] An impressive proof of the greater male ability to think abstractly is that among the current eighty-two grandmasters at chess not a woman is to be found, although there are a lot of female chess players, especially in the Soviet Union. There has never been a woman grandmaster, and among the five hundred best chess players of all time there is not one woman.[105] The fact that all significant mathematicians *without exception* have been men points in the same direction.

The man's greater strength in abstract reasoning certainly does not mean that the man is more intelligent than the woman, for abstract thinking is only one *aspect* of intelligence. Moreover the usual intelligence tests show that as regards total intelligence the sexes are not really different.[106] In addition, it is impossible to determine intelligence completely objectively. For on the one hand the scientific concept of intelligence rests on the input of those who define it, and on the other it is questionable whether human intellectual abilities can in general be reduced to measurable data. An intelligence test can recognise only certain very real aspects of the human intellect, but there are others which escape quantifiable measurement. For example, it is impossible to quantify outstanding creative achievements in painting, music or literature. That is not to contest the value of intelligence and aptitude tests, but to note their limitations. But one thing can definitely be affirmed on the basis of test results so far. Exceptionally high scores are reached by more men than women, while among low scorers more men are represented than women.[107] So it is not surprising that the most brilliant achievements in the realms of philosophy, art, and musical composition and the pioneering discoveries in modern science are either exclusively or overwhelmingly the work of men.[108] This also goes for literature, though on average women have a higher linguistic aptitude. Invention is also predominantly a male preserve. In one period among fifty-four thousand registered patents only six came from women.[109] The realm of genius and intellectual innovation is therefore obviously a male domain.

To point out the lack of educational opportunity in the past for women does not suffice to explain this state of affairs. For even in those periods in which women had relatively easy access to education (e.g., the twentieth century, the Roman Empire or the early Middle Ages) the total picture does not really change. Male spontaneity and female receptivity, discussed in the preceding section, have their spin-offs in the intellectual realm. Whereas the man is well known in his thinking to be the more creative, the woman is known to be more receptive when it comes to thought. This is confirmed by aptitude tests which have shown male superiority when it comes to 'comprehension and reasoning', while 'women excel in all rote-learning tasks'.[110] Even in pre-school years boys show 'greater creativity and originality'.[111] So it could be said that male intelligence compared with female is productive or creative, whereas female intelligence is rather receptive or reproductive. An illuminating illustration of the intellectual differences between the sexes comes from the early Middle Ages, a high point for education in convents. Then the learned medieval women, in contrast to the learned men of the Middle Ages, did not come up with their own research and new results, but fulfilled the task of 'mastering the received intellectual heritage and passing it on'.[112] Something similar may be observed in music. While women have often proved to be outstanding musical interpreters (*e.g.*, pianists), the creation of great compositions has been reserved exclusively for men.

The more creative character of male intellectual life and the more receptive female aspect is of profound significance for human culture. The poetess Gertrud von le Fort sees the reception of intellectual cultural achievements as the special and irreplaceable task of women. For her the woman is the preserver and keeper of intellectual values, whereas she sees the man as the creator of culture who needs woman to receive his work. 'To give without being received would be to fall into a void. Culture does not just need to be made, it needs carrying, protecting and loving like a child.'[113] The woman is specially equipped to give herself in service to others, and to understand and to mediate between what is given and human beings,[114] that is, to realise mankind's intellectual values. The woman brings about this connection of intellectual values and concrete human life particularly as the mother of her child:

> The mother, who teaches the child the first sounds of language . . . , who sings to him the first songs of his people, who tells him his first fairy tales, she represents the first and most decisive cultural factor in the child's life, the earliest influence on his intellectual life. It is of immeasurable importance, not just for the child but for the culture.[115]

Male intellectual achievement can be understood as an intellectual fatherhood analogous to his physical fatherhood. This is suggested in English when we talk of Wernher von Braun as the father of space travel or Edward Teller as the father of the hydrogen bomb. Conversely, the female spirit which receives, preserves and links up with the spirit of life represents one part of her intellectual motherhood and corresponds to her biological motherhood. Fatherhood and motherhood are distinctive marks of men and women that determine not only their physical but also their intellectual life.

The greater intellectual creativity of the man is matched by the greater involvement in life of the woman.[116] This greater life-involvement is seen in the intellectual realm in the greater concreteness and experience-relatedness of her thinking.[117] The woman's thinking tends towards the visible and particular, whereas the man's is more strongly directed towards the conceptual and general.[118] For men this carries the danger that their reflection may become autonomous and cut off from the real world. It is very well known that eccentricity is much more often met with in men than in women.[119] Knowledge for the woman consists not just in an immediate relationship with concrete visible reality but also in a closer contact with her emotional life.[120] There are indications that this fact, which is constantly observed in everyday life, is based on the particular brain structure of women and not on socially conditioned custom.[121] The woman is in comparison to the man the more holistic being.[122] She is in less danger than he is of isolating her soul from her body or her thinking from her feelings. The body and the emotional life play a greater role in her life than in a man's.

Conversely, a woman's thinking compared to a man's plays a lesser role in the totality of her psychic life – which of course must not be misunderstood as a lesser capacity for thought.[123] 'The woman experiences herself more as a whole being than the man does. She reacts to any stimulus in a more lively and complete way than the man.'[124] It has long been established that the woman's being is more dominated by her feelings than the man's. This view of woman's special emotionality corresponds not only to widespread prescientific conviction, but has been proved scientifically.[125] For example, it has been experimentally demonstrated that women have a preference for the emotional.[126] Whereas men tend to underrate feelings or even write them off altogether, girls and women rate feelings highly.[127] Even among pre-school children, girls exhibit a more finely tuned and more highly differentiated emotional life than do boys.[128] A woman's feelings show a greater sensitivity and sensibility than the man's.[129] This is associated with the greater sensitivity of her skin and its enhanced responsiveness to the pleasures of touch.[130] It also reflects her greater closeness to life, and the more intimate connection between her psychic life and her bodily processes.[131] For feeling is the function of the human soul which, when it becomes conscious, is in most immediate connection with the body. The profound impact of the emotions on breathing, heart rate, muscles and digestion, to name just a few examples, is as obvious as the strong dependence of the emotional life on bodily conditions.[132] The connection between soul and body is much closer in women than in men, so that consequently emotion plays a greater role in a woman's life than in a man's.

The greater sensitivity of women gives a special degree of empathy with other people's character and needs.[133] The woman has therefore with some justice been called 'Nature's psychologist'.[134] 'She feels and guesses rightly where the man often only touches and goes wrong.'[135] Even young girls show 'a much more refined and developed identification with the situation of others' than young boys do.[136] Study of girls' essays as opposed to boys' showed a greater emotional richness and a greater ability 'to sympathize with others'.[137] The woman's special ability to sympathise proves itself in an unsurpassed way in being a mother. Max Scheler points out that

the vital psychic unity between mother and child established in pregnancy is not completely severed by the organic separation of their bodies. The mother carries around with her a sort of organic system of signs of her child's life which gives her a more profound knowledge about her child than is accessible to anyone else.[138]

As the woman's body adapts in an amazing way to the needs of the sucking infant, so the woman's soul adapts in a unique way to the child's needs. The woman's special gift of sympathy stands in a very intimate relationship to her maternal task. It is a mark of her real motherliness, which she can confirm and develop even if she is denied children of her own.

In close connection with her gift of sympathy is the woman's particular 'sociability' (*i.e.*, the tendency to seek the company of others and take pleasure in it) and her stronger drive to serve (*i.e.*, the tendency to give others help and support when they are in trouble).[139] These properties also belong together with motherhood to constitute the being and destiny of the woman. The strong drive to serve in the female may be observed from the age of three or four:

> Girls tend to perform a care-taking and protective role; they often play with children younger than themselves, whom they help and assist, while boys tend to play with older children and to join in their activities. These behaviour patterns are characteristic not only in our society; they have also been found in infants and young children belonging to cultures as varied as India, Okinawa, Mexico, Kenya, and the Philippines.[140]

The woman's special willingness and ability to care is backed up by her greater adaptability, which is likewise noticeable in childhood.[141] This is basically a consequence of the female ability to sympathise. From sympathy for the needs of others grows the ability to adapt to them appropriately.

Closely connected to woman's adaptability is her greater readiness to submit to the leadership of others, while in the man there exists a distinctly greater tendency to leadership (dominance).[142] The male tendency to direct and lead is a fact observable in all cultures.[143] It is already apparent in boyhood, but particularly after puberty,[144] and in sexual union it is symbolically expressed.[145] The man's propensity for leadership is closely connected with his greater aggressiveness, which is already recognisable from the age of three.[146] This explains the fact that crimes of violence are almost exclusively male offences. The man's greater aggressiveness matches his bodily build, which is particularly equipped to overcome resistance in his environment and to remodel it creatively or destructively.

Our description of the intellectual–psychological differences between the sexes has shown how different the sexes are, not just physically but also intellectually and psychologically. In the following section we want to attempt to bring together what has been said hitherto into a total picture which focuses on the different outlooks of the sexes.

3 The Different Outlooks of the Sexes

To be a man or woman is more than the sum of particular sex-determined characteristics. We must therefore try to build up a complete picture in which bodily and psychological gender-determined characteristics are arranged coherently.

The point of view that brings together the various individual differences between the sexes is their differing attitude to the world. The man has a closer relationship with the world of things, whereas the woman has a closer link with the world of persons.

The more intimate relationship of the man to the world of things is apparent in his total psychosomatic constitution, as we have depicted it in the preceding chapters. The man's body is equipped for the practical remodelling of the environment (*cf.* his bone structure and his muscles). His greater ability in abstract and spatial thinking compared with the woman's also allows him to master mentally the world of things, and this provides the intellectual foundation for its practical reordering.

While the woman's body is in large measure built for bearing and bringing up children, the man's, as far as bearing and bringing up children are concerned, is equipped simply to enable the all-important but brief moment of generation. The man's existence is obviously not centred on the personal duty of bringing up children. The man's intellectual creativity, particularly expressed in the great intellectual achievements and scientific discoveries, shows the man's more developed relationship to the world of things.

The woman's more developed relationship to the world of persons is expressed in her whole psychosomatic constitution. Her body is less fitted for remodelling the environment than for protectively and lovingly arranging her surroundings, which is vital for the well-being and security of mankind. Her body is also well-equipped for motherhood, for carrying, giving birth to, caring for and bringing up children. The woman's body is an inescapable pointer to the way her being is orientated towards people. Her greater linguistic aptitude also destines her to relate to people, for speech serves interpersonal understanding and creates human society. The woman's particular fluency shows that she is specially equipped to communicate with other people and that she has a closer relationship to the world of persons. When compared with men the woman's greater sensitivity, empathy, adaptability, her more developed concern to serve and her motherliness show how much closer the woman stands to the world of people than to the world of things.

The different outlooks of men and women are confirmed by the results of psychological research into their interests. Relying on Kampmann's material, we shall now demonstrate this.[147] Investigation into children's games has shown that boys have a particular interest in competitive or technical games, whereas girls prefer family games.[148] Girls' games, in contrast to boys', always revolve round people. 'For the boy what matters is his relationship to the facts of the game, for the girl, though, what matters is the personal relationship.'[149] This fundamental difference of interest in games, which is discernible in the pre-school years, is also very clear at school. 'Twelve-year-old girls already show an astonishing capacity to appreciate other people and a marked interest in interpersonal relationships.'[150] An investigation of reading interests in puberty showed that 'encounters with men and love scenes were the consuming interest of girls'.[151] 'Accounts of all female readers leave no doubt that they are interested only in the description of interpersonal relations, particularly those between the sexes.[152] Round about fourteen years old boys prefer to read adventure stories or historical narratives, whereas girls show much more interest in short stories and novels.[153] Among adults women enjoy novels much more than men do.[154] One can aptly sum up the results of this research as follows: 'The woman is always interested in the personal realm, her own person, then what is close to her in time and space, in fact in everything that belongs immediately in her orbit.'[155]

This conclusion is confirmed by pictures produced by children: 'Boys prefer to depict the external world with its means of transport; girls, however, the home and its people.'[156] The woman's stronger relationship with people is also seen in her greater openness to being influenced by others. Much educational experience has shown that the person of the teacher has far greater significance for girls than for boys, and that goes as much for the teacher's achievements as for his interests.[157] The woman shows a much greater tendency 'to adopt interests pursued by the loved one'.[158] All this demonstrates that the greater attachment to things in the man and the greater involvement with people in the woman is confirmed by psychology.

The different outlooks of men and women are thus of great moment for their gender-specific tasks. The greater interest in external things equips the man for involvement in the world; the deeper relationship with people destines the woman to the task of being man's companion and motherhood.

4   The Relative Independence of Gender Differences from the Environment

The psychosomatic gender differences are so well known and assured by so many scientific investigations that no serious person can contest them. However it is maintained again and again, particularly by feminists, that these determinable differences in the psychosomatic realm are exclusively or predominantly conditioned by society. So we want now to look at the significance of environment and education on the differences between men and women.

To trace psychological gender differences exclusively back

to the social environment founders on the body–soul unity of man. For if a person is a real unity of body and soul, it is impossible to ascribe a totally asexual psyche to a sexually determined body. Rather, because of man's psychosomatic unity, a sexually determined mind–soul must be assumed. Since, then, the sexual character of the human body is hardly dependent at all on the environment, one must infer a psyche which within certain limits is independent of the environment. Human mental and spiritual life has at any rate a life of its own over against the scarcely influenceable character of the body. The relative independence of the mind–soul rests on its capacity for self-determination, to think, will and act on its own. This possibility of free self-determination makes man special over against the animal world. Human freedom involves the possibility that someone may think and act against their own nature, so that a dualism of body and soul may result. But this possibility is not unlimited, since a person is bound to their body and can only live to a certain extent in contradiction to it. For human sexuality this means that a person has a limited freedom to live and act in defiance of their sexually determined psychosomatic individuality. It is therefore possible for a man consciously to behave in an unmanly fashion or a woman to act in an unwomanly way. Perversions such as homosexuality are a sad proof that a person can deny and be false to their sexuality. As far as cultures are concerned, there are those which allow the development of the sexual individuality of men and women and there are those that suppress it. It therefore makes sense to speak of cultures or periods as masculine- or feminine-shaped. The Enlightenment period because of its over-emphasis on reason could be called a masculine era, whereas the Romantic era with its overemphasis on feeling could be termed a feminine one.

In the light of human freedom and the possibility of degenerating in unnatural ways, it is no surprise that various cultures and societies have different conceptions of what it means to be male or female – a subject well documented with convincing examples by the anthropologist M. Mead.[159] That is in no way to assert that the sexual individuality of a man or a woman allows no freedom for a man or woman to develop their maleness or femaleness. There are various ways of realising male or female existence (*e.g.*, inside and outside marriage). Strictly speaking one must say: to be a man or a woman is always something quite individual, never something schematised. For the man or the woman does not exist in general, but always only as a particular man or woman with quite individual gifts and limitations within which they develop as male or female.

This freedom of movement is of course limited. When sexes deny or suppress their natural male or female individuality, they rebel against their nature and their destiny and mistake their sexuality. In this case one can and must speak of degeneration. It is all a matter of making sure that a person's way of life is consonant with their particular sexual endowment, for only then do they use their own sexuality rightly and live as is appropriate to their male or female nature. In this connection it is, incidentally, not advisable to talk of innate male or female characteristics, for the human properties which determine behaviour are not given complete at birth, but they result from an educational process through which the endowment which underlies these properties unfolds. It is therefore more exact to talk of an innate gender-specific endowment. The intellectual-psychological gender differences are neither simply innate nor simply a product of the environment, but they are the result of innate gender-specific endowments which are developed or suppressed by environment and upbringing. The intellectual–psychological gender differences are therefore primarily conditioned by the endowment and only secondarily by the milieu. The milieu must therefore start with the given, that is with the person's innate constitution, and can only influence this positively or negatively, but cannot creatively reverse it. The environment's possible influence is thus firmly limited by a person's given constitution.

Our conviction about the primacy of the innate (*i.e.*, the

endowment-conditioned individuality of men and women) is confirmed by a multitude of research results. For example, brain research in the last twenty years has brought out clear indications that the man's more developed spatial-reasoning ability and the woman's greater linguistic aptitude rest on their different brain structures.[160] Furthermore, the closer connection of thought and emotion in women and also the outstanding achievements of men in certain specialised intellectual realms seem to be related to the different constitution of their brains.[161] Genetic research has also produced evidence of the primacy of endowment over environment. For example, a long series of experiments suggests that spatial conceptual ability is hereditary.[162] The same goes for the man's (on average) greater mathematical ability: 'In all contexts sons show on average higher mathematical gifts than daughters. This suggests that there is something in women hampering, and in men something encouraging mathematical ability.'[163] According to Möbius there is not a single known case where 'mathematical talent has been inherited from the mother'.[164] With mathematically gifted women, 'the talent, in so far as its genetic roots are traceable, comes from the father'.[165]

Hormone research also confirms the innateness of gender-specific aptitudes and modes of behaviour. A connection between hormones and spatial-conceptualising ability[166] is just as assured as between hormones and the male tendency to dominance and aggression.[167]

In the light of the results of brain, genetic and hormone research it should come as no surprise that even in infants there are discernible differences between the sexes. For example, the greater female receptivity and involvement with people can already be observed in infants. According to Restak, girls soon after birth 'are more receptive towards certain sounds, especially their mothers' voice' than are boys.[168] 'In general they pay more attention to people around them, faces, ways of speaking and slight changes of voices. At five months a girl can distinguish photos of people she knows, which a boy of this age rarely can.'[169]

Baby boys relate markedly less clearly to people. In contrast to girls, at five months they 'cannot distinguish between a face and a swinging toy. They react just as quickly to a lifeless object as to a living person.'[170] We see in all this that the different outlook on the world of the sexes shows in infancy and is not just the result of a specific upbringing.

Research on pre-school children also confirms the dominance of innate ability over environment. An investigation of the Ko-bushmen showed that there were characteristic differences between the sexes in games and drawing, although there 'was no social pressure whatsoever on children in a specifically male or female direction'.[171] The observations of the well-known psychologist Christa Meves confirm that behavioural differences between the sexes are primarily due to innate abilities.[172] A striking confirmation of this is the fact that there are worldwide agreements about the image of the sexes in the most different cultures. The American Steven Goldberg has demonstrated in a thorough study (described as convincing by the famous anthropologist Margaret Mead[173]) that throughout the world, past and present, there has never existed a society in which the overwhelming majority of key positions in state, industry and society were not occupied by men. In other words, and contrary to the opinion of many feminists, there is nowhere evidence of a matriarchal society (that is a society led by women).[174] All supposed examples, which some researchers have adduced for the existence of matriarchy, do not hold up when subject to closer scrutiny.[175]

Goldberg demonstrates further that in societies past and present the generally dominant conviction is that the man should lead and have authority in marriage, family and society.[176] In fact men, as Margaret Mead says, 'have always been leaders in public affairs and the final authorities in the home'.[177] This fact is primarily to be ascribed to the hormonally conditioned tendency of men towards direction and leadership, not to environmental influence. Goldberg's proof of universal expectations about the sexes and behaviour patterns offers ethnological confirmation of the thesis that it is not the environment but innate attributes which are primarily responsible for the appearance of differences between the sexes.

To conclude: we may regard the primacy of endowment over environment as established through the body-soul unity, through brain, genetic and hormone research, and through behavioural studies and ethnology. Significant deviations from gender-specific behaviour are adequately explained by people's capacity to flout their nature and predisposition. All this leads to a decisive consequence for educational practice: any education that forgets or attempts to iron out the gender-determined character of men and women is directed against human nature and inevitably must be destructive. The same is true of any attempt to achieve self-fulfilment without regard to one's sex and to the limitations which that imposes. It is not difficult to see that this cuts the vital nerve of the feminist movement, for it stands and falls with the conviction that the sexes do not differ in their fundamental nature, but only in a few bodily differences which have little or no effect on the psyche.

5   Theological Consequences

Quite deliberately we restrict ourselves to a very brief theological comment on the results of our analysis of gender-related differences, as the centre of our research is the biblical material and its consequences for the present. The final authority for Christian conviction and behaviour can never be scientific study, which is always open to revision. The final authority is rather Holy Scripture, which as God's revelation discloses deeper truths than the most solidly based science ever can. That is not to undervalue science, as proud Christians have done again and again, for true science can help the believer to a deeper grasp of divinely revealed truths. As our study proceeds we shall see how well the biblical and scientific views of the sexes complement and confirm each other.

The first important conclusion to be drawn by Christians from the scientifically established differences between the sexes is that God has created men and women to be different, because he has *different purposes* for them. For the character of the sexes is not the chance result of blind evolutionary processes, but the product of a consciously planned creative act of God. Everything God calls into existence, including human sexuality, springs from a profound divine purpose and serves his glorification. The sexes therefore have the task of realising God's creative purpose and thereby glorifying him. That means thankfully accepting their sexuality and consciously developing it. Each person is called to a life consonant with their creation. When someone rails against God's creation, he destroys himself. When the sexes rebel against their created nature and seek to deny it, they rebel against the living God and allow their life to be destroyed. In an age of the direst perversions in the realm of sexuality Christians are called to live as men and women in God's intended way and prove it to be a source of deepest happiness.

By looking at Christian men it should be apparent that it is a joy to be a man, and Christian women should show the joy of being a woman. The Holy Spirit wants to help us realise God's creative purpose for the sexes with happiness. So we intend in the next chapters to listen to the biblical view about male and female and thereby establish standards for our life as twentieth-century Christians.

Before closing this long section on sexual differences, we should say something about the limitations of our knowledge about men and women. However full and well-founded our knowledge of gender differences, a Christian knows that he is barred from a total rational knowledge. God's wisdom which shines out in all his work is always greater than we can grasp as limited human beings. A deep mystery hangs over male and female, which drives us to adoration. All our knowledge about the sexes remains necessarily partial (*cf*. 1 Cor 13:9), even if modern scientifically minded man will not accept this. For Christians, however, the knowledge that there are ultimate mysteries is no stumbling-block, but a motive for praise of the unimaginably rich wisdom of the creator, 'who does great things and unsearchable, marvellous things without number' (Job 5:9).

5

Man and Woman in the Old Testament

1 Man and Woman in Genesis 1–3

Genesis 1–3 are the most fundamental chapters about man and woman in the Old Testament. They also constitute an indispensable presupposition for the New Testament view of the sexes, a presupposition which is explicitly confirmed and deepened by the Christian revelation. Because of the supreme importance of these first chapters of the Bible for the New Testament we want to concentrate our description of the Old Testament view of male and female on these chapters and outline only briefly the rest of the Old Testament teaching. Three basic ideas will serve as keys in studying biblical texts about the sexes: the affirmation of sexuality, the equality of the sexes, and the assumption of the differences between man and woman.

Before we begin the study of Genesis 1–3, a few observations on the character and interpretation of these chapters are indispensable. Genesis 1–2:4 is the account of the creation of the world, Genesis 2 describes the creation of mankind, and Genesis 3 the fall. All three chapters are composed in poetic language. The common assumption in Old Testament scholarship that Genesis 1 comes from a different source from Genesis 2–3 is of no real significance for our study. The attempt of some exegetes to demonstrate a real theological difference or indeed contradiction between Genesis 1 and the following chapters is not convincing. We shall show in our study of Genesis 1–3 that they agree on the main points and that they complement each other fruitfully.

In this connection it is of decisive importance that we read Genesis 1–3 in two ways. On the one hand the chapters report something that happened in the past (*e.g.*, the creation and the fall of man); on the other they make statements about our present situation (*e.g.*, about man and sin). What happened in the fall of the first human pair reflects the danger to and the sin of mankind today. The story of the fall is therefore both an account of a past primeval event and also an illustration and mirror of present human sinfulness. So Genesis 2 does not make statements just about the relationship of Adam and Eve, but simultaneously it makes fundamental statements about male and female which claim to be fully valid for the present as well. This intertwining of 'factual report',[178] which of course must not be misunderstood as an exact historical report, and statements about present reality run through the whole narrative of the creation of man and the fall.

A fine example of the switch from a report about the past to a fundamental statement about mankind is in Genesis 2:23–4. Genesis 2:23 portrays Adam's excitement when he first saw Eve. Genesis 2:24 draws out from this the truth still valid today: 'Therefore a man leaves his father and mother and cleaves to his wife, and they become one flesh.' Immediately the report about Adam and Eve resumes, '[They] were both naked . . .' This example shows clearly the fusion of statements about the past and the present.

In our analysis of Genesis 1–3 we shall try to be faithful to this mixture of historical truth and permanently valid truth within the texts. But of course the emphasis will be placed on the fundamental statements about men and women that are still valid today.

a   The Affirmation of Sexuality

The report on the creation of the world in Genesis 1 reaches its climax in the creation of man: 'So God created man in his own image, in the image of God he created him; male and female he created them' (Gen 1:27). This verse affirms human sexuality to be something given from the beginning, and indeed a human characteristic which was intended by God. God did not create man as a sexless spirit, but as male and female. The statement of verse 27 receives additional weight through verse 31: 'And God saw everything that he had made, and behold, it was very good.' To be a man or a woman is therefore to enjoy God's whole-hearted approval. Men and women are 'very good' in God's eyes and therefore must be accepted by humanity as 'very good' too. Verse 28 puts the physical aspect of human sexuality under God's special blessing: 'And God blessed them, and God said to them, "Be fruitful and multiply, and fill the earth . . ."' Offspring, a goal of human sexuality, is the fruit of divine blessing and an outworking of God's plan.

Genesis 1 is free of all types of antipathy to the body which devalue it as the animal side of man or despise it as the prison of his soul (cf. Plato). The affirmation of human sexuality, of corporeality, and of sex is so unrestrained that it cannot be exceeded. For what greater can be said about the sexes than that they are the realisation of the very good thoughts of God? The Old Testament scholar Claus Schedl is therefore perfectly correct to say, 'If ever a total "yes" to sexuality was spoken, then it was in the creation account.'[179] The history of Christendom shows sufficiently how uncertain the total 'yes' to sexuality has often been among Christians.[180]

It is tragic that this first chapter of the Bible experienced an interpretation that turned its affirmation of man as a sexual being into the opposite. As late as this century there have been exegetes who have understood verse 27 to express the creation of an androgynous first being, that is a male-female dual creature. This interpretation translated the end of the verse as follows: 'God . . . created it [mankind] as male-female.' If this interpretation were correct, it would have severe consequences for the understanding of mankind and its sexuality. The sexually determined person would not then correspond to the original divine intention, but would be a later development labouring under the suspicion that he or she is merely a degenerate form of the original human being.

In fact exegetes who started with the idea of an androgynous being have posited a primeval fall whereby the human being sank into physical sexuality. Theodor Böhmerle, for example, saw the primeval fall as consisting of Adam 'instead of carrying the female principle within him, wanting to have it beside him. In that direction lay a false, anti-God solution of the feminist problem, and thereby the whole destructive stream of sin's corruption was let loose.'[181] Even more bluntly Theodor Culmann maintained: 'The creation of woman is such a fearful catastrophe, only exceeded by death itself, whose forerunner she is.'[182] It is obvious that such an interpretation must lead to an antipathy to the body and a devaluation or denial of human sexuality.[183]

This interpretation which has just been outlined is untenable for three reasons:

1. Genesis 1:27 says explicitly: 'God created . . . them [not him] male and female.' Gerhard von Rad rightly says that the plural 'them' 'prevents one from assuming the creation of an originally androgynous man', since the preceding singular form 'God created *man*' leads one to expect a singular 'him' here.[184] At the same time the expression 'them' shows that the usual translation 'God created them as man and woman' is fully justified in fact, and that it aptly represents the sense of the Hebrew text's 'male and female', though it is not a literal translation.

2. The parallel passage Genesis 5:2 confirms our interpretation, for there too the plural form 'them' instead of 'him' is found ('Male and female he created them, and he blessed them . . .').[185]

3. Genesis 1:28 unequivocally disproves the assumption that verse 27 speaks of an androgynous human being: 'God blessed *them*, and God said to *them*, "Be fruitful and multiply . . ."' Both the plural ('them') and the demand to produce descendants only make sense when God is dealing not with a bisexual individual, but with a human pair.[186]

The idea of an original androgynous man is not of biblical, but of clearly heathen origin. It is found in Plato,[187] in Philo,[188] a philosopher influenced by Platonism, and in Gnosticism.[189] The non-Christian conception of androgynous humanity gained influence over some church fathers (*e.g.*, Gregory of Nyssa[190]) and especially in the theosophical school of thought of Böhme, Oetinger, J. M. Hahn, de St Martin, Franz von Baader, Soloviev and Berdyaev,[191] without ever establishing itself in the church. Happily it remained a fringe phenomenon within Christianity.

The uninhibited affirmation of sexuality in Genesis 1 is also found in Genesis 2: the creation of the woman is greeted with shouts of joy by the man (Gen 2:23) and is regarded by God as the *completion* of his human creation, which is not good without the woman (Gen 2:18). Not until there are two sexes is the situation reached in Genesis 2 that Genesis 1:31 describes as 'very good'. Genesis 2:24 regards man and woman becoming 'one flesh', in a psycho-spiritual and sexual union, as a divinely willed goal of creation. Genesis 2:25 emphasises that Adam and Eve were naked without being ashamed. This innocence of paradise expresses clearly the untroubled and unconditional 'yes' of the first human couple towards their sexuality. So, like Genesis 1, Genesis 2 is free of every kind of disapproval or devaluation of the sexual.

b The Equality of the Sexes

The first chapters of Holy Scripture are informed by the conviction that the sexes are equal before God. A particularly impressive witness to the equal worth of men and women is Genesis 1:27: 'So God created man in his own image, in the image of God he created him; male and female he created them.' Men *and* women are here dignified with being God's image. Neither sex has an advantage which makes it more valuable than the other. In Genesis 1:27 'the equal worth of the sexes is emphasised: both together constitute the human species'.[192] In Genesis 1:27 it is evident that 'the idea of man . . . finds its full meaning not in the male alone but in man and woman' together.[193] According to Genesis 1, humanity comes into existence in both the man and the woman, which both represent equally valuable manifestations of humanity. Genesis 1:27 is the permanently valid biblical 'no' to the devaluation of women in whatever form this appears. Woman possesses the full dignity of the image of God. Verse 27 could be paraphrased: 'And God created man and woman in his image, in the image of God he created them.'

Does the image of God ascribed to human beings relate also to their sexuality? Are men and women the image of God only in regard to their common human nature, or do they also reflect God's nature through their sexual distinctiveness? In what follows we shall try to answer these questions, as we clarify what the concept 'image of God' means.

First, it should be pointed out that in the original Hebrew two different words are used, 'image' (*selem*) and 'likeness' (*demut*). Both words have roughly the same meaning. *Selem* (image) mostly means 'sculpture', 'statue' or 'shaped image'; it is thus always a description of a material image. Whereas *demut* (likeness) is a term of comparison, which presupposes the similarity of one thing to another and like *selem* may be translated 'image'.[194]

Whether both terms are translated 'image' or 'representation' or whether the sense of 'image' should be distinguished from 'likeness' is irrelevant to the meaning of this verse. Both words attest 'a correspondence between man and God',[195] a unique comparability of humanity with God, which rests on a real similarity between creator and creature. Genesis 1:27 expresses the special place of humanity in all creation. In the statement about humanity's divine image 'the total superiority of man over the animal . . . is summed up'.[196] 'Humanity is not made according to the measure of the animal, but according to the measure of God himself . . .'[197] Genesis 1:27 does not say only that man is created *according* to God's image, but *as* the image of God, for image means something tangible, the image of something else.[198] Man is the image, 'precisely the embodiment of God within creation'.[199]

Is this statement still true for humanity after the fall? Certainly sinful man cannot be seen as God's image in the same way as he was before the fall. But equally certainly, the similarity to God mentioned in Genesis 1:27 is not simply lost in the sinner. Passages like Genesis 5:1 and 9:6 make it clear that mankind after the fall still has the image of God (*cf.* Ps 8).

So what precisely does the image of God consist of? The context of Genesis 1:27 gives an important clue to answering this question. In verse 28 God commits authority over all creation to humanity: 'And God blessed them, and God said to them, "Be fruitful and multiply, and fill the earth and subdue it; and have dominion over the fish of the sea and over the birds of the air and over every living thing that moves upon the earth."' The image of God in man and dominion over creation clearly stand in a close relationship to each other. Man reflects the lordship of God, in that he himself is lord over the earth. Of course that does not mean that the image of God in man is identical with man's lordship over creation, it is rather the presupposition for his rule:[200] because man is the image of God, he is capable and equipped to rule the earth. Man is created as God's image irrespective of whether his rule over creation is just or not. The statement about the image of God describes in the first instance not a task, but an essential aspect of humanity, from which certain quite distinct tasks flow, tasks which are compatible with being in God's image. So the divine commission to rule the earth is to be understood as an appropriate material expression of the image of God given to man.

If the image of God is the presupposition of man's commission to rule, it seems likely that it should be associated with his mind and soul, with his capacity for thinking, willing and acting, which represents the necessary presupposition of his rule over creation. This is in fact in the history of interpretation the commonest understanding of our passage.[201] In its favour there is the illuminating insight that man, precisely through his mind, through being a person, reflects the personality of God and is qualitatively different from the animal kingdom. God's personhood expressed in his thinking, willing and acting has its image in man's personal thinking, willing and acting. In passing, the idea that man could through his material body portray God's totally immaterial being appears quite misguided.

However, this interpretation is not wholly satisfactory.

Dillmann in his commentary pointed out that the human mind cannot be separated from the body in this way:

> In so far as this intellectual nature [of man] gives to his external appearance the honour and dignity (beautiful form, upright posture, commanding bearing) that distinguish him from all earthly creatures . . . his bodily shape, the expression and instrument of his spirit, is not to be separated from his intellectual nature. So it should certainly not be excluded from the idea of the image of God.[202]

One can only concur with this view, for it conflicts both with the wording of Genesis 1:27 and the Old Testament view of man to relate the image of God in man solely to his mind-soul. In Genesis 1:27 it is not the human soul, but man that is described as the image of God – even though there is no precise equivalent in Hebrew to mind (the closest would be the Hebrew term, *leb*, 'Heart'). The term man (*adam*) always means in Hebrew the whole man, who as a whole is God's creation and cannot be envisaged without a body. Also verse 27 includes the corporeality of man, for it refers to human sexual differentiation (male and female). It cannot therefore be said 'that only the mind is created in God's image. Man . . . bears God's impression as a totality, as a body-soul being.'[203] He is, as a whole, God's image.

This has consequences for our initial question whether the image of God also relates to his sexuality. Since sexuality involves the whole person it is likely that it should be connected with his being in the image of God,[204] the more so because Genesis 1:27 explicitly speaks of being male and female. However, one must proceed very cautiously in attempting to answer the question. In what way do man and woman reflect God? For on the one hand our text says nothing about it, and on the other the fact that the whole person reflects God in no way means that the person reflects God in every aspect. The human being is not only God's image but is also a creature of God, and is in that respect bound much closer to the creation than to the creator.

Although, then, his body belongs to the divine image, in

that it makes possible human life, thought and action, man's material form is not the divine image, for God's existence is totally independent of a material body. Genesis 1:27 speaks not only of a relative similarity between God and man (the image of God) but also of an absolute dissimilarity, namely of the irremovable difference between creator and creature. We must therefore always ask in what respect man reflects God and in what respect he does not, in which way human sexuality is an image of God and in which it is not. In posing this question we have left the realm of the exegesis of Genesis 1:27 and have entered the realm of systematic theology. We cannot answer the question of how far male and female reflect God in their sexual nature through further exegesis of Genesis 1, but only through a systematic theological investigation built on the total witness of Holy Scripture (see Chapter 10, section 4). But we can affirm as a secure result of our exegesis that male and female are understood in Genesis 1 as equally in the image of God, and every form of the devaluation of woman is thereby categorically rejected.

In Genesis 2 the equality of the sexes is clearly expressed. Verse 18 states: 'Then the Lord God said, "It is not good that the man should be alone; I will make him a helper fit for him."' The woman is here termed as man's helper, and more precisely as a helper 'matching him'. Gerhard von Rad has correctly pointed out that the expression 'matching him' involves both 'the notion of similarity as well as supplementation',[205] that is of an equal but different partner. The equal worth of the sexes comes even more clearly to expression in verse 23, where the man hails the wife created for him with a 'jubilant welcome':[206]

> This at last is bone of my bones
>   and flesh of my flesh;
> she shall be called Woman,
>   because she was taken out of Man.

The words translated 'Man' and 'Woman' are based on a play on words in the original Hebrew, namely *ish* (man) and *ishshah* (woman). 'The choice of these expressions indicates that this creature has the *same nature*, (*ish*) as the man, but is different from him, see the ending *ah*.'[207] The term *ishshah* for the woman 'expresses both the equality and the different nature'.[208] The naming of the woman shows how deeply the man feels that she is an equal and a partner of identical worth.

The equality of the sexes is underlined by the following verse: 'Therefore a man leaves his father and his mother and cleaves to his wife, and they become one flesh' (v. 24). The becoming 'one flesh' expresses the equal partnership of man and wife, 'their personal community in the broadest sense, . . . bodily and spiritual community, mutual help and understanding, joy and contentment in each other'.[209] Genesis 2:24 is free from every devaluation of woman: 'She is obviously so precious to her husband, that he leaves his dearest, his family, for her sake.'[210] The weight of verse 24 can only be adequately understood when it is seen against the background of the high value placed on parents and family in the Old Testament. Here the wife is valued even more highly than the husband's family, which was so highly respected in Israel! The wife is the husband's most precious partner who cannot be displaced by anyone (whether ancestor or descendant). The one-flesh union, the most perfect and most intimate form of human fellowship, is only possible between husband and wife. Clearly, Genesis 2:24 is dealing with monogamy: it only mentions explicitly one man and one woman who become one flesh. Even if the verse does not directly speak of marriage as a life-long institution, its phraseology is totally incompatible with (misogynous) polygamy. It refers only to monogamy.

These few observations should be sufficient to show how free Genesis 2 is from any devaluation of women. It is no surprise that the Old Testament scholar Claus Westermann concludes that Genesis 2 is unique in its high valuation of women 'among the creation myths of the whole of the Ancient Near East'.[211]

c   The Differences Between the Sexes

Genesis 1–3 confirms that the nature, place, and function of the sexes are fundamentally distinct. Genesis 1 emphasises that God created humanity male and female, without specifying more precisely where the differences between the sexes lie. That sexuality is mentioned in the fundamental verse about the image of God in man indicates that maleness and femaleness are not secondary but are an important feature of human existence. Genesis 2 and 3 then explain in detail what the natural differentiation between the sexes consists of. These chapters offer a more precise illustration of the importance of the two sexes for mankind. In what follows we shall try to make clear those truths about the differentiation of men and women which are addressed in Genesis 1 and 2.

A lovely testimony to the fundamental difference between the sexes is Genesis 2:18: 'Then the Lord God said, "It is not good that the man should be alone; I will make him a helper fit for him."' The verse speaks explicitly of the man's need of help, the state in which he finds himself without a wife as his match. The man is portrayed as a being in need of help and completion, who desperately requires a wife. Without a wife the man is in an unsatisfactory situation, which does not enjoy the total approval of God. Only with the creation of a wife is the unsatisfactory situation of man relieved and a state produced that deserves the verdict 'very good' (Gen 1:31).

With a wife, the 'help' is there to complete man just where he needs it. It diminishes the text if the idea of help is limited to the process of procreation, in which the woman conceives, carries and gives birth for the man. Dillmann rightly observes that in verse 18 there is no talk of procreation.[212] Just as becoming one flesh (Gen 2:24) does not just mean sexual union but the total personal fellowship between husband and wife, so the term 'help', which Luther aptly translated 'helper', describes the comprehensive help, both physical and spiritual, that the husband experiences through his wife.

Even though it is not explicitly put into words here, our verse does not speak only of the completion of the man by the wife, it also presupposes that the wife experiences help and completion through her husband: God does not create a complete person as a match for man, but he creates a person who is to complete the man, not a further human development to replace the man. Genesis 2:18 is a denial of every concept of a perfect person who needs no further completion. If it is not good for the man to be alone, it is also not good for the woman to be alone. Both sexes need completion and help from each other. Genesis 2:18 shows that there are real differences between men and women. These serve to supply the lacks and needs of the one sex through the gifts of the other.

The difference in nature between men and women becomes clear in Genesis 2 in the different way God creates them. The man is formed out of the earth (v. 7), but woman is created out of man's rib (vv. 21–2). The different ways of creating man and woman are closely related to their different tasks, which they fulfil in creation according to Genesis 2–3. The man is formed from the soil, whose cultivation is entrusted to him by God (Gen 2:15; 3:17), while the woman is created quite differently, out of man's rib, to be his helper. This is her God-given task in life (Gen 2:18). The appointed tasks of the sexes are as basically different as the ways in which they were created by God. Their different modes of creation are intimately related to their tasks in life. It is worth noting that Genesis 2 and 3 in their own language make clear the very different world-outlooks of the sexes, which we have already met in the anthropological–psychological part of this book (Chapter 4, section 3). While the man has an immediate relationship to the world of things, the woman is primarily directed to the world of persons (*i.e.*, in the first instance to her husband).

Further investigation of Genesis 2 and 3 confirms this interpretation. In addition to the man's task of food production through cultivating the ground and the woman's task of being man's helper, another task of the man and the woman is mentioned which confirms the greater thing-related outlook of the man and the stronger personal attachment of the woman. In Genesis 2:19–20 the man is commissioned to name the animals. Giving a name is more than labelling: it is 'an act of appropriate ordering, by which a man intellectually objectifies the creatures for himself'. It is an 'act of recognition and interpretation that takes place in language'.[213] It involves organising conceptually the space which surrounds Adam. According to ancient ideas 'the nature of something is expressed by its name'.[214] Naming the animals helps to achieve a mental grasp of their character. It is 'only the actual expression of a previous inward interpretative appropriation'.[215] We see this very well in Adam's inventing of the words *ish* for man and *ishshah* for woman, which expresses both the difference in nature between the sexes as well as their similarity.

It is striking that the man is entrusted by God with naming the animal kingdom (*i.e.*, with comprehending the living world that surrounds him). In this way the theoretical task of comprehending his environment is added to the practical task of transforming the world. The man is given by God the task of mentally comprehending and practically transforming the world. Subduing the world, which was the commission given to man at creation according to Genesis 1:28, does not consist merely in making it subject to and useful for humanity, but also in its intellectual subjection. Naming is in ancient Near Eastern ideology the 'exercise of sovereignty, of command'.[216] In naming the animals Adam fulfils part of his commission to subdue the earth (Gen 2:18). It is no coincidence that Adam, not Eve, is entrusted with naming the animal kingdom. God wants to enable Adam not only to comprehend his environment intellectually, but to lead him to self-understanding, to realise that he needs the woman as a helper. So the report of naming the animals concludes with the sentence: 'The man gave names to all cattle, and to the birds of the air, and to every beast of the field; but for the man there was not found a helper fit for him' (Gen 2:20). Through understanding the animal kingdom Adam discovered that his isolation and need for help could not be solved by a non-human creature.

The extent of Adam's commission to comprehend his environment appears not only in the charge to name the animals, but in his reaction to the creation of woman. His astonished shout is not just a joyful reaction, but an intellectual summary of the nature of male and female:

> This at last is bone of my bones
> and flesh of my flesh;
> she shall be called Woman,
> because she was taken out of Man.

It is noteworthy that even here the man himself grasps the new situation, and that God himself does not introduce the woman to the man nor does she introduce herself. It is also not by chance that God informs the man, not the woman, of the prohibition not to eat of the tree of knowledge (Gen 2:16–17). In all this we see that God entrusted the man with the task of intellectually comprehending the world. Thus Genesis 2 and 3 attest in their own way the closer psychological relationship of the man to the world of things and physical relationships.

The greater personal interaction of the woman is visible in the second responsibility assigned to her in Genesis 2 and 3 alongside her appointment as man's help: motherhood is a further significant responsibility of woman in Genesis 3:16. Admittedly this verse deals with the execution of the divine sentence on the woman following the fall and not with formulating the responsibility itself. But the verse does presuppose motherhood and subordination to the man, just as the sentence on the man presupposes his responsibility to provide food. Both the sexes are affected in their principal responsibilities by the divine judgement. To be man's helper and a mother are according to Genesis 2 and 3 the fundamental responsibilities of the woman. Both are person-related responsibilities and exemplify the greater personal interaction of the female. Here it is worth noting that the primary responsibility of the woman is not said to be motherhood – which might be expected given the extraordinarily high valuation of motherhood in Old Testament Israel – but to live life as the man's partner!

Genesis 2 and 3 shed new light on Genesis 1:28's command to mankind to be fruitful and subdue the earth. Although this task is given to man and woman, as the wording of Genesis 1:28 makes clear, its fulfilment imposes different obligations on the sexes, as we can see from Genesis 2 and 3. While the woman as mother is entrusted more with the duty of propagating the human race, the man is particularly entrusted with subduing the earth; Genesis 2 makes this clear through his responsibility to cultivate the earth and name the animals. So man and woman together fulfil the divine commission, each contributing in the way appropriate to their sex. The Catholic philosopher and nun Edith Stein has appropriately described the different participation of the sexes in the divinely appointed task: 'In the man the call to rule is primary, whereas fatherhood is secondary. (It is part of ruling, rather than being subordinate to or an adjunct to it.) In the woman the maternal call is primary, and sharing the rule is secondary (it is partly included in mothering).'[217]

We can conclude that Genesis 2 and 3 express clearly the natural differentiation of men and women and suggest correspondingly different responsibilities for the sexes. Finally we want to note the different attitudes of the sexes to each other as they emerge in Genesis 2 and 3.

The man according to Genesis 2:18 is the origin and goal of the woman. Woman is taken out of man and created for him to complete him and to help him. This relationship is not reversible. 'That original creaturely "from there" and that original "for the sake of" applies only to the woman. A reversal of this relationship does not apply!'[218] Genesis 2:18 not only expresses the sexes' mutual need of completion and help but also a non-reversible orientation of the woman towards the man as the reference point for her life. Claus Westermann rightly insists: 'One could not say in [Genesis] 2:18 that man is created as a helper for the woman.'[219] Paul aptly sums up the content of Genesis 2:18 in the sentence: 'Neither was man created for woman, but woman for man' (1 Cor 11:9). The description of the man in Genesis 2 does not start with the woman, but the woman's description starts with the man. This is connected with the man being set over the woman. For if the woman has the responsibility to assist the man in his God-appointed responsibilities, that means that the woman has to be subject to the man. Gertrude Reidick correctly recognises this when she writes: 'As regards that fellowship of man and woman in which she ought to stand by him, she occupies a secondary position; for whoever helps does not lead but offers support, accompanies, offers advice and action, but does not take the initiative.'[220] The Lutheran systematic theologian Peter Brunner is quite right when he finds the content of the New Testament view that man is the 'head' of the woman (1 Cor 11:3) already in essence present in Genesis 2:18.[221]

Other passages in Genesis 2 and 3 confirm that the leading role is attributed to the man whom the woman as a person of equal worth should stand by to give help to and support.[222] Edith Stein sees implied in the fact that 'the man was created first . . . a certain primacy'.[223] It is at any rate striking that in Genesis 2 and 3 the man is viewed as God's primary partner in conversation. It is the man (not the woman) whom God addresses about his moral responsibility towards God. After the fall God first summons Adam, not Eve, although she led him into sin, 'Adam, where are you?' (Gen 3:9). Adam received the divine command not to eat of the tree of knowledge, and he is therefore in a special way responsible for upholding it. Eve, however, learned of the divine command only indirectly through Adam, not from God himself. That is why Adam and not Eve was first called to account by God. Adam in both Genesis 2 and 3 is addressed as the one to whom God has entrusted the responsibility of spiritual leadership. His is the responsibility to instruct Eve in the divine commandment and to make sure that neither she nor he transgress it. Martin Luther has beautifully portrayed Adam preaching to his wife in paradise.[224] Even if we should abstain from such speculative portrayals, one can still say: 'From the garden of Eden story onwards Adam, not Eve, is put forward as preacher and guardian of the divine word.'[225]

The great fault of Adam in the fall was his denial of

responsibility for spiritual leadership, and instead of submitting to God's command submitting to his wife's leadership. So God begins his sentence 'Because you have listened to the voice of your wife' (Gen 3:17). The sin of Adam therefore consists not just of disobeying God, which is of course decisive, but in the perversion of his created situation *vis-à-vis* Eve. He committed himself to her religious initiative and leadership instead of maintaining his own responsibility for leadership as God intended. The fall is therefore not only the rebellion of mankind against God, but the setting aside of the divinely appointed order of male and female. The Old Testament scholar J. T. Walsh has drawn attention to this point. In a valuable analysis of Genesis 2–3 he shows that before the fall there are four levels of authority (God—Man—Woman—Animal). In the fall this is inverted into precisely the opposite. The snake (representing the animal kingdom) gains authority over the woman, the woman authority over the man, while God's authority is suppressed through the influence of the snake.[226] The English theologian Gordon Wenham aptly sums up the sinful reversal as follows: 'Eve listened to the serpent instead of Adam: Adam listened to Eve instead of God.'[227] *After* the fall God reinstates the original structure of authority when he puts the snake under the woman, the woman under the man, and all three under his divine authority.[228] The fourfold hierarchy of Walsh is so obvious that it cannot seriously be contested. That God represents the supreme authority needs no discussion. That the animal kingdom is subject to man is shown (apart from Gen 1:28) by man naming the animals, which discloses his authority over them (Gen 2:18–19). That the woman is subject to the man is clear not only in Genesis 2:18, but also in Genesis 2:23, where the man expresses his superiority over her by naming her. Of course in this fourfold grading of authority the steps in the hierarchy are in no way equal. God's authority stands absolutely over all other levels. The authority of mankind over the animals is essentially different from the authority of the man over the woman, which only consists of the right to lead in a partnership of equals.

Walsh's four-level hierarchy in Genesis 2 and 3 confirms the insight already reached that in both chapters the man is placed over the woman and appointed by God to lead. This is of great significance in understanding the fall. The leadership position of the man makes him specially responsible for the transgression of the divine commandment.[229] P. Brunner concludes, not without reason, 'that the fall is made final by the man's action. Only by the man's deed does the fall become ripe for judgement . . . It is true that Adam is deceived by Eve, but the fall is completed by Adam.'[230] The leadership position of the man intended by God in Genesis 2 precludes ascribing to Eve the chief guilt for the fall, as has happened time and again in the Judaeo-Christian tradition. His seduction by Eve offers no excuse for Adam, for he was pledged on the basis of his spiritual responsibility to correct his wife and to prevent the disobedience initiated by her from turning into joint rebellion against God.

The story of the fall is of abiding significance for us as it allows us to recognise the special risks facing men and women. It is an unmistakable warning of the danger which arises if the woman seizes the religious leadership that God has entrusted to the man. Eve's misadventure begins with her forsaking the spiritual leadership of her husband and involving herself without him in a dialogue with the snake (Gen 3:1–5). The story of the fall consists of two distinct scenes.[231] In the first scene the conversation takes place between the woman and the snake (Gen 3:1–5). There is no mention of the man. His absence is obviously presupposed, for it explicitly says: 'The serpent . . . said to the *woman* . . .' The first scene creates the inner predisposition in the woman to transgress God's command in the given situation. Only in the second scene, where there is no more talk of the snake, does Eve covet directly to eat of the tree of knowledge: '. . . the woman saw that the tree was good for food, and that it was a delight to the eyes, and that the tree was to be desired to make one wise . . .' (Gen 3:6). The conversation with the snake sowed the seed for the transgression of the divine commandment. Now the seed sprouts, and Eve succumbs to the temptation: '. . . She took of its fruit and ate . . .' (Gen 3:6).

Before the conversation with the snake there was no incentive to despise the divine commandment. Now, after the conversation, the temptation is there. The text no longer presupposes that the snake is present, but, in contrast to the first scene, it does presuppose the presence of the man: '. . . and she also gave some to her husband, and he ate.' In both scenes Eve is the one who takes the initiative, while Adam appears just a passive onlooker who willingly lets his wife lead. It is obvious that at the fall the woman ruled over her husband and instead of being his helper to live as God intended, led him into evil. So quite rightly Edith Stein states that the woman 'in tempting the man put herself over him'.[232]

Straight after the fall God corrects the woman by explicitly endorsing the man's dominion: '. . . and he shall rule over you' (Gen 3:16). We shall look more closely at the interpretation of this controversial passage in Excursus 2. For our present discussion it suffices to establish that God sharply rejects the dominion and leadership of the woman that was apparent in the fall. The story of the fall shows that the woman fundamentally endangers herself and the man by her bid to dominate. But to maintain the divinely intended order of the sexes, as it appears in Genesis 2, is a protection against evil for both sexes. The reversal of this order makes both hostages to evil and brings destructive consequences. The story of the fall thus sheds new light on the divine ordering of the sexes. The divinely intended subordination of the woman has nothing to do with the oppression of women by men, but is a beneficial arrangement that protects men and women from the destructive power of evil. The woman runs into great danger when she steps outside this protective ordinance. The story of the fall shows the woman as a creature in special need of protection and particularly open to Satanic seduction. As many commentators have noted,[233] it is not by chance that the snake goes to the woman. The snake addresses her because she 'is more receptive of new impressions'.[234] Gerhard von

Rad sees in the seduction of the woman by the snake and the consequent seduction of the man by the woman an indication that the woman 'confronts the obscure allurements and mysteries which beset our limited life more directly than the man does. In the history of Yahweh-religion it has always been the women who have shown an inclination for obscure astrological cults.'[235] This interpretation is not an exegetical fancy. There are in the Old Testament (*cf.* Exod 22:18; 1 Sam 28:7–25)[236] and in anthropology[237] serious hints that women are more open to the occult than men. This fits in with the fact that women have greater receptivity than men. They are therefore more liable to be affected by their surroundings. This characteristic of women is neutral in itself and can be used for good or ill. However, it was exploited by the snake. At the beginning of the history of condemnation stands the misuse of female receptivity. At the climax of salvation history God used female receptivity to make the incarnation of his Son possible. The receptive 'Let it be to me according to your word' (Luke 1:38) of Mary brings salvation to all humanity, just as Eve's misuse of receptivity brought condemnation to all. The greater receptivity and openness to influence of the woman which the snake exploited shows her particular need of help which her subordination to man serves. Placing the man over the woman in Genesis 2 is therefore a blessing which serves her good. It is a helpful ordinance for both sexes. The story of the fall shows that to upset this order ends in catastrophe for both sexes.

There are commentators who understand women's subordination to the man to be a result of the fall, arguing that it does not correspond to the original will of God.[238] They appeal to Genesis 3:16, where God sentences the woman to be subject to the man. In that case it would be a punishment not a blessing. We want to examine in the following excursus the sense in which God's word to the woman, '. . . he shall rule over you', is to be understood.

Excursus 2
The subordination of the woman in Genesis 3:16

However Genesis 3:16 is to be interpreted, at least our treatment certainly shows that those interpretations are untenable which maintain that Genesis 2 affirms a total equality of rank between the sexes and that the subordination of woman is first addressed in Genesis 3:16. Our study of Genesis 2 and 3 has shown that the man is placed in authority over the woman in being given responsibility for leadership. The subordination of the woman is thus not a punishment caused by sin, but a creation ordinance that expresses God's will for the sexes. The equal worth of men and women according to Genesis 2:18 and other passages is not to be confused with their equal rank, but it includes a super/subordination of equally valuable partners.

To be taken more seriously than the first type of interpretation is the idea that the woman's subordination in Genesis 2 is intensified into oppression by men in Genesis 3:16 as punishment for her sin. So, for example, Calvin writes in his commentary on Genesis: 'She had, indeed, previously been subject to her husband, but that was a liberal and gentle subjection; now she is cast into servitude.'[239] But it must be asked whether Genesis 3:16 can really mean that God nullifies the relationship between the sexes of Genesis 2 and *ordains* a despotic rule of man over woman. The text gives no warrant for holding that God imposes a punishment involving male tyrannical oppression of the woman or that it regards such despotism as good. The Jewish exegete Jacob has raised a telling objection: 'If the woman were now punished with subjection under the man, he would be given an advantage which he least deserved at this moment.'[240] Attempts have been made to get round these difficulties by seeing Genesis 3:16 not as proclaiming a divine punishment but only a divine announcement.[241] So Genesis 3:16 should not be translated 'He *shall* rule over you' but 'He *will* rule over you.' So, for example, Hick insists

> that the text merely expresses the fact of the man's rule even under the changed circumstances. It does not give a right to rule in an authoritarian way, and it certainly imposes no duty to do so.

It therefore follows that the woman is not burdened with a new duty of obedience. On the contrary the existing subordination (*cf*. Gen 2) continues in force despite the changed situation.[242]

According to this interpretation God does not alter the creation ordinance of Genesis 2 to the woman's detriment, but announces to the woman what she will have to suffer in the way of oppression by men. In favour of this interpretation it may be argued that it takes Genesis 3:16 seriously as a word of judgement without drawing untenable conclusions from it, either that the subordination of the woman originates as punishment for the fall or even that it justifies male oppression of women.

There is also an interpretation of Genesis 3:16 which holds that it just expresses what is already in the creation ordinance of Genesis 2. This interpretation is for example advocated by Thomas Aquinas,[243] Luther,[244] and in our century by the Jewish exegete B. Jacob.[245] For it a whole series of arguments may be adduced.

1. The wording of Genesis 3:16 does not demand a negative interpretation, in which a despotic rule is presupposed. The Hebrew word for 'to rule', *mashal*, may describe a negative oppressive rule, but it may be used in an explicitly positive sense. For example, the Old Testament uses it for God's rule (*cf*. Isa 40:10; Ps 22:28), or of the eschatological reign of the Messiah (*cf*. Mic 5:1ff).[246]

2. In Old Testament thinking man's rule and the subordination of women is not something negative. It is therefore questionable to start out with modern presuppositions and see Genesis 3:16 as bemoaning the oppression of women. Westermann correctly insists that the 'situation of the woman' in the Old Testament was not felt to be ' "degrading" because of the domination of the husband, but only when she has no children or when she does not belong to any husband'.[247]

3. The suggested interpretation makes a plausible connection between Genesis 3:1–6 and Genesis 3:16. The woman broke loose in the fall from subordination to the man (Gen 3:1–6), and for this reason is explicitly redirected by God to the place that suits her in creation (Gen 3:16).

4. The wording of Genesis 3:16 does not at all warrant the conclusion that the order of the sexes in Genesis 2 has fundamentally altered. The wording gives no scope for questioning that man is the origin and goal of the woman or that she is his helper.

5. Though Genesis 3:16 is a sentence on the woman, this does not mean that all its statements are punitive in character. The remark

'he shall rule over you' is only one part of Genesis 3:16 and need not necessarily be a punishment, but it could be a summons to return to the creation subordination to the man (*cf.* point 3). Genesis 3:16 contains at least two remarks which in no way involve punishment. The remark that the woman will bear children is not punitive, only the accompanying circumstances of birth are punishments for the fall. Nor is the remark that the wife will long for her husband a punishment. This deals with a fact of the created order which is in no way negative but is related to woman's relationship to man in Genesis 2. That her desire for the man is not negative is shown by Genesis 2:24, where the same is said about the man: the man leaves his parents because he longs for a wife. So we see that the punitive character of Genesis 3:16 does not mean at all that the subordination of the woman must be a punishment.

6. In 1 Corinthians 14:34 Paul respects Genesis 3:16 as a still valid divine ordinance.[248] Since everywhere else Paul always appeals to Genesis 2 in establishing his position about men and women (except for 1 Tim 2:13), it shows that he does not regard Genesis 3:16 as an innovation conditioned by the fall, but a creation ordinance. If Luther's basic principle is taken seriously, that 'Holy Scripture is its own interpreter', 1 Corinthians 14:34 must certainly be drawn on for understanding Genesis 3:16.

I leave the reader to choose which interpretation to adopt. But in our view there are only two worthy of serious consideration. Either Genesis 3:16 ordains only that subordination of women to men which is already part of God's creation ordinance in Genesis 2. Or Genesis 3:16 states that woman will be oppressed by men as a result of her sin, without justifying such oppression. At any rate it is quite untenable to understand Genesis 3:16 as proof that the subordination of women to men is a punishment or curse because of the fall.

---

2   Man and Woman in the Rest of the Old Testament

a   The Affirmation of Sexuality

The affirmation of the sexuality and physicality of human beings is not only found in Genesis 1–3, but characterises the whole Old Testament. It is impossible to cite here all the texts which attest this. We must therefore restrict ourselves to a few. An eloquent testimony to the wholehearted 'yes' to human sexuality is, for example, Proverbs 5:18–19 (NIV):

> May your fountain be blessed,
>   and may you rejoice in the wife of your youth.
> A loving doe, a graceful deer –
>   may her breasts satisfy you always,
>   may you ever be captivated by her love.[249]

This passage attests such a joyful affirmation of sexuality that many readers will probably be surprised to find such a remark in the Bible at all.

A high point in the Old Testament affirmation of the sexual is the Song of Songs, which in an unsurpassed way portrays the beauty and joy of love between man and woman. The bridegroom's description of the charming bride in Song of Songs 4:1ff. attests the high value put on physical beauty:

> Behold, you are beautiful, my love,
>   behold, you are beautiful!
> Your eyes are doves
>   behind your veil.
> Your hair is like a flock of goats,
>   moving down the slopes of Gilead . . .
> Your lips are like a scarlet thread,
>   and your mouth is lovely.
> Your cheeks are like halves of a pomegranate
>   behind your veil . . .
> You are all fair, my love;
>   there is no flaw in you. (Song 4:1, 3, 7)

Even Ecclesiastes, where so much is said about the misery and pointlessness of human existence, says, 'Enjoy life with the wife whom you love, all the days of your vain life which he has given you under the sun' (Eccl 9:9). This explicit affirmation of married love has its impact on Israel's law. According to Deuteronomy 24:5 the married man is legally

exempt for a year from military service and similar duties, 'to
be happy with his wife whom he has taken'.

These passages should suffice to demonstrate the affirmation of the sexual throughout the Old Testament. The Old
Testament believer knew that he owed his entire being,
including his sexuality, to the wonderful wisdom of his
creator:

> I praise you because I am fearfully and wonderfully made;
>   Your works are wonderful,
>   I know that full well. (Ps 139:14, NIV).

b   The Equality of the Sexes

A recognition of the equal value of the sexes appears in many
Old Testament passages. There is a whole series of laws in
which men and women are given equal status. Exodus
21:28ff., for example, threatens with death the owner of an ox
who has been warned and has taken no precautions, if his ox
gores a man or a woman to death. If however a slave or slave
girl dies, the owner must pay just thirty shekels. This example
shows not only how different is the standing of freemen and
slaves, and freewomen and slave girls, but that in both cases
the sexes are treated as legally equal. The same goes for that
provision which makes a capital offence the striking or
cursing of the mother as well as the striking or cursing of the
father (Exod 21:15, 17; Lev 20:9). This is the more notable
when one observes that according to Babylonian law the
striking or cursing of the mother was not punished.[250] In the
Old Testament the father and the mother have an equal 'right
to love, honour and obedience from their children . . . There
is no difference here.'[251] This is made clear by the fifth
commandment in the decalogue, 'Honour your father and
your mother, that your days may be long in the land which the
Lord your God gives you' (Exod 20:12; cf. Deut 5:16). The
high place of women in the Old Testament is evident from the
fact that in twenty-eight cases of naming children it is done by
the mother, and in only eighteen cases by the father.[252] This
all shows the high status the woman enjoyed as mother.

To this should be added the strikingly high status of the married woman. The hymn to the good wife in Proverbs 31:10–31 is indicative:

A good wife who can find?
　　She is far more precious than jewels.
The heart of her husband trusts in her,
　　and he will have no lack of gain.
She does him good, and not harm,
　　all the days of her life . . .
She opens her mouth with wisdom,
　　and the teaching of kindness is on her tongue . . .
Her children rise up and call her blessed;
　　her husband also, and he praises her . . .
Charm is deceitful, and beauty is vain,
　　but a woman who fears the Lord is to be praised.
　　　　　　　　　(Prov 31:10–12, 26, 28, 30)

Also in religion there is a recognition of the woman's equality.[253] Not just men, but also women enjoy personal religious experiences (e.g., Judg 13:3ff.; Gen 16:7ff.; 21:17) and answers to prayer (cf. Gen 25:21; 1 Sam 1:18–20); they participate in such important events as the bringing up of the ark to Jerusalem (2 Sam 6:5, 15, 20) and the worship led by Ezra after the return from exile (Neh 8:2); they take part in worship and religious festivities, especially in the passover at home (Exod 12:3ff.) and in offering sacrifices (Judg 13:23). Women, like men, could swear oaths in God's name (Ruth 1:17) and could take the Nazirite vow of spiritual consecration (cf. Num 6:2). The law basically applies to both sexes (cf. Deut 29:10ff.). The law is therefore read to both men and women (Deut 31:12; Josh 8:35; Neh 8:2–3). So instruction in the law involves not just sons but also daughters (Deut 11:19, 21).

The prophetic office is in no way restricted to men. The Old Testament tells of significant prophetesses such as Miriam (Exod 15:20), Deborah (Judg 4:4; 5:7), Huldah (2 Kings 22:14), and Noadiah (Neh 6:14). These indications should suffice to show that the equality of the sexes was recognised in ordinary life and in religious affairs. However, we must draw attention here to the fact that a series of passages express a devaluation of women and put them at a disadvantage (*cf.* here section d below).

c   The Differences Between the Sexes

The Old Testament takes for granted the differentiation of male and female. This is seen in religious and in ordinary life. For example, women, unlike men, were not obliged to go on pilgrimage to the three great feasts of Israel held in the temple (*cf.* Exod 23:17; 34:23; Deut 16:16–17). The most significant difference between men and women in religion consists of restricting the priesthood to men in contrast to the practice of the surrounding oriental world (Exod 28–29; Lev 8–9). The priestly office covered not just sacrifice but also the author-ised exposition of the law (Lev 10:11). This corresponds completely to the spiritual leadership position of the man in Genesis 2 and 3, which we were able to establish in our investigation.

Also in ordinary affairs the man was given the responsi-bility of leadership. The man was obliged to undertake the defence of the common life and to care for the defence of his wife and family (*cf.* Isa 4:1). The wife on the other hand had charge of the home and its affairs. In bringing up children, which was jointly undertaken by father and mother, she was primarily entrusted with the young children and with the daughters, while the man had much more to do with the older children and especially with the sons.[254] The man was generally regarded as head of the family, as the one who had final authority in making decisions (*cf.* Exod 21:3, 22; Deut 24:1–4).[255] His authority over the woman was expressed in the title *adon*, that is 'lord' (*cf.* Gen 18:12; Judg 19:26–7), or *ba'al*, 'lord' or 'owner' (*cf.* Gen 20:3; Exod 21:3, 22), which his wife used to address him. One might be tempted in the light of the term *ba'al* to interpret the woman's position as like that of a slave. But this title does not express 'a slave relationship, for a slave girl does not call her master *ba'al*'.[256]

Neither does the title *adon* ('lord') imply that the wife is in a slave relationship to her husband. It is true that *adon* correlates with *ebed*, 'slave', and *ama* or *shifha*,'maid', but the title *adon* is not used only in the context of slavery, but also as a term of respect for those one wants to be polite to.[257] The term *adon* may be used in addressing a father, a brother, or an uncle or even people of lower status.[258] When an Israelite wife called her husband *adon*, she was expressing her respect for him, not that she was his slave.

To sum up. In Old Testament Israel the different responsibilities of man and wife as they are set out in Genesis 2 and 3 (with the man as leader and breadwinner and the wife as companion and mother) were seen as valid in both the religious and the secular realm. However, the social *practice* in ancient Israel in no way matched the relation between the sexes of Genesis 2. The equality of the woman as man's partner expressed there, although taken into account in the legal and personal sphere (see section b above), was rendered partially ineffective through a socio-legal undervaluation that placed women at a disadvantage (see section d below).

d   The Oppression of Women

The generally high place given to women in the Old Testament was spoiled by legal rules and by traditions which led to their oppression and denied their equality.

Legally the man counted as the 'owner' of the wife (*cf.* Exod 21:3, 22; Deut 24:4; 2 Sam 11:26), and the woman as her husband's 'possession' (Gen 20:3; Deut 22:22).[259] The bridegroom had to make a marriage payment to the bride's father (Gen 34:12; Exod 22:17; 1 Sam 18:25). This sealed the betrothal and established the legal rights of the bridegroom.[260] The Hebrew word for 'betroth' really means 'legally make one's own'.[261] The marriage which follows betrothal is correspondingly an act in which the man takes possession of the wife (*cf.* Deut 21:13; 24:1).[262] Although this point must not be overrated, as other laws do maintain the wife's dignity as a person, it is obvious that such classification of her as property does totally contradict her valuation as the equal partner of her husband in Genesis 2. The same goes for polygamy, which was legally permitted in Israel (*cf.* Lev 18:18; Deut 21:15). It clearly contradicts Genesis 2:24, which speaks of *one* man and *one* woman as partners in the divinely willed sexual relationship. However, it must be pointed out that monogamy was the normal type of sexual partnership in Old Testament Israel.[263]

Another example of the legal disadvantage of being a woman is seen in the rules about divorce and adultery. While the man was permitted a divorce under certain circumstances (*cf.* Deut 24:1), the woman had no right to divorce. Whereas a man was guilty of adultery only when he had intercourse with a married or betrothed woman (*cf.* Deut 22:22–29), any wife having sex outside her marriage counted as adulterous. A husband could not therefore commit adultery against his own marriage partner, only against someone else's.[264] Also in the laws of inheritance the woman was disadvantaged. 'Daughters had no claim to inherit, if there were sons.'[265]

All these examples show that the undervaluation of women and discrimination against them in the Old Testament had not been fully overcome. Despite this one must admit in the light of the mass of Old Testament evidence for the high valuation placed on women that (as Döller concludes) 'Without doubt the woman in Israel had a status found among few other peoples.'[266]

6

Man and Woman in the Teaching of Jesus

1 The Affirmation of Sexuality

Jesus' proclamation expresses an unconditional 'yes' to human sexuality. We see this most clearly in Matthew 19:3–9 and Mark 10:6–9, where Jesus expressly accepts the affirmation of sexuality found in Genesis 1 and 2. Jesus replies there to the question whether a man may leave his wife for any reason. He begins his reply by pointing to Genesis 1:27 and Genesis 2:24: 'Have you not read that he who made them from the beginning made them male and female, and said, "For this reason a man shall leave his father and mother and be joined to his wife, and the two shall become one"?' (Matt 19:4b–5). This remark of our Lord rules out any interpretation that reads into Genesis 1:27 the creation of a bisexual (androgynous) human being.[267] Matthew 19:4 (as in Gen 1:27) speaks literally not of 'man and woman' but of 'male and female'. This phrase has misled some to ascribe to Jesus the idea of an originally androgynous being.[268] But the wording and context of the verse make this interpretation impossible: Jesus (like Gen 1:27) uses the plural 'them', whereas on the androgynous interpretation the singular 'him' would be expected. Jesus explicitly emphasises that human beings were created *from the beginning* male and female, so that there was never an original state in which man was a bisexual creature. Sexuality is therefore God's most original purpose in creation.

In Matthew 19:5 Jesus makes it absolutely clear that he knows of no androgynous original state of man. Since he links

Genesis 2:24, which speaks incontrovertibly of two sexes, directly with Genesis 1:27 (Matt 19:4), he shows that Genesis 1:27 speaks of the polarity of the sexes and not of an originally bisexual person. Thus in Matthew 19:4–5 Jesus underlines emphatically that human sexuality, including the sexual union of man and wife, corresponds to God's perfect creative purpose. It is therefore understandable why Jesus' proclamation is completely free from any contempt or disparagement of sexuality. That cannot be a surprise, for Jesus' incarnation (becoming human) involves an unreserved affirmation of sexuality. Since Jesus appeared as a *man* on earth, maleness is confirmed to be a divinely ordained state; and since Jesus was born of a *woman*, that shows that womanhood enjoys God's favour too.

Jesus' attitude to sexuality completely corresponds to the Old Testament affirmation of sexuality. However, Jesus does not simply repeat the Old Testament outlook, he introduces a new standpoint: Jesus speaks in Matthew 19:11–12 of the possibility of celibacy for God's sake. Such a possibility is foreign to Old Testament thought. The Old Testament presupposes that the affirmation of sexuality involves its exercise within marriage. Celibacy appears as shameful (*cf.* Isa 4:1) and contrary to creation (*cf.* Gen 1:28). 'Not to be married is a disgrace, because it means that a man is prevented from realising a complete life.'[269] Jeremiah shows that it was possible to embrace celibacy in response to God's call (Jer 16:1ff.), but this did not remove the painful stigma of the unmarried life (Jer 15:17–18). Whereas in Jeremiah's case celibacy was viewed negatively, as a warning of imminent divine judgement, Jesus sees celibacy as something positive, which may advance God's kingdom. The celibacy spoken of by Jesus in Matthew 19:10ff. 'is a voluntary renunciation . . . which for the sake of God's kingdom, proved necessary in his service',[270] a renunciation through which God brings perfection. Matthew 19:10ff. shows that for Jesus sexuality should be completely subservient to God's rule, which has arrived in his person (*cf.* Matt 12:28 and parallels, Matt 11:14–15; Luke 17:20–1).

According to Jesus, God is sovereign over creation and

therefore God's kingdom is sovereign over human needs (*cf* Matt 4:1–11; 6:33). Jesus does not thereby retract his unreserved affirmation of sexuality, expressed a few verses earlier, but he subordinates sexuality to the great goal of his mission, the establishment of God's rule. A renunciation of marriage for God's sake does not at all mean a devaluation or abolition of sexuality, but only the renunciation of physical involvement out of love for God and humanity, a love which Jesus regards as the 'law of life under the reign of God'[271] (*cf.* Matt 22:34–40 and parallels; Matt 7:12). Sexuality thus remains fundamentally significant even for Jesus' unmarried disciples, for in Jesus' view the sexes, whether they are married or not, each have their part to play in building the kingdom of God, parts which are distinct and correspond to their sexual natures.

For Jesus' attitude to sexuality Matthew 22:23–33 (and parallels) is of great importance. There Jesus goes into the question of what will become of the sexes in the future divine world. In order to understand it better we quote him in full:

[23] The same day Sadducees came to him, who say that there is no resurrection; and they asked him a question, [24]saying, 'Teacher, Moses said, "If a man dies, having no children, his brother must marry the widow, and raise up children for his brother." [25]Now there were seven brothers among us; the first married, and died, and having no children left his wife to his brother. [26]So too the second and third, down to the seventh. [27]After them all, the woman died. [28]In the resurrection, therefore, to which of the seven will she be wife? For they all had her.'

[29]But Jesus answered them, 'You are wrong, because you know neither the scriptures nor the power of God. [30]For in the resurrection they neither marry nor are given in marriage, but are like angels in heaven. [31]And as for the resurrection of the dead, have you not read what was said to you by God, [32]"I am the God of Abraham, and the God of Isaac, and the God of Jacob"? He is not God of the dead, but of the living.' [33]And when the crowd heard it, they were astonished at his teaching.

For us the crucial question is, Does Jesus here speak of a complete abolition of both sexes in the state of perfection, or should the passage be understood differently? Jesus' reply to the Sadducees at least affirms that, in God's eternal world in which mortality and death are abolished, sex, procreation and the bodily kind of existence necessary for procreation will cease. In the Lukan parallel Jesus expressly mentions the immortality of the blessed which makes marriage and procreation unnecessary: '. . . they cannot die any more, because they are equal to angels' (Luke 20:36). The Catholic theologian Franz Zimmermann sees in this explanatory remark about the immortality of the perfected a proof that our text is dealing with the process of procreation and is saying only that 'sexual intimacy with the purpose of procreation ends for the resurrected, because it has no further point [*i.e.,* because they are immortal].[272]

The creation commission for man to procreate is therefore valid only for God's first creation; it does not apply in the perfect eschatological new age. Whether with the abolition of marriage and procreation the psychological aspect of sexuality is also abolished cannot be deduced from the text. Jesus is not discussing the question whether humanity's sexually determined character persists in another, unimaginable way in the resurrection. The Catholic New Testament scholar Peter Ketter therefore supposes, 'By His answer to the Sadducees Jesus did not mean to convey the impression that all difference between the sexes ceases in heaven.'[273] Against the assumption that after the resurrection human sexuality is completely put aside it may be objected that the redeemed retain their identity in their resurrected state. And sexuality is inseparable from a person's ego. One might further object that the New Testament attests a resurrection of the *body* (*cf.* 1 Cor 15). Disputing with heretics, the church fathers Augustine and Jerome already emphasised that the resurrection involves the body, and that includes 'sexual particularity'.[274] This fits in with the fact that the resurrected Jesus in the Easter accounts appears, albeit in a transfigured mode of existence, as a *man* and not as an asexual or bisexual hybrid.

According to Zimmermann the eradication of sexuality would be incompatible 'with the principle that God does not hate anything he has made'.[275] Further, Jesus' remark that the perfected will live 'like the angels' must not be understood as a promise of an asexual final state, for angels according to the Bible have a sexually determined appearance (*e.g.*, Dan 8:15; 9:21; Luke 24:4).[276]

In all this we see that there are serious reasons for the assumption that the dual sexuality of mankind continues in God's eternal realm, even though neither Matthew 22:23–33 (and its parallels) nor other passages in the New Testament address this question directly.

2   The Equality of the Sexes

Jesus bore witness in a striking way through his life and message to the equality of the sexes. His attitude to women is quite unique, so that it stands in stark contrast to the misogynist practice of contemporary Judaism.[277] Before we examine more closely Jesus' dealings with women, we intend to clarify the position of women in first-century Judaism, since it is only against this background that the extraordinary attitude of Jesus emerges clearly.

Excursus 3
The position of women in Judaism at the time of Jesus [278]

The position of women in Judaism at the time of Jesus is far less favourable than in Old Testament times. Whereas the Old Testament contains significant evidence for the equality of the sexes and the high valuation of women, in later rabbinic Judaism an obvious devaluation of women had set in. In some instances this can only be described as misogyny. For example, the Jewish writer Josephus (AD 37–100) writes that the woman is 'in all things inferior to the man'.[279] One of the rabbis said: 'Happy is the man who has male children, woe to him who has female children.'[280] Rabbi Judah said

(c. AD 150): 'A man must pronounce three blessings each day "Blessed be the Lord who did not make me a heathen . . . blessed be he who did not make me a woman . . . blessed be he who did not make me an uneducated person".'[281] Women were placed by the rabbis on the level of lowly valued children and slaves.[282] The low status of women is also seen in the rabbinic interpretation of the fall: Eve is portrayed as the chief culprit, who brought corruption on all mankind.[283] The cited passages, which could easily be multiplied, give some impression of the widespread low status of women in Judaism at that time.

This low status is also apparent in social and religious life. Rabbi Jose ben Yohanan of Jerusalem (c. AD 150) advised: 'Talk not much with womankind.'[284] Later wisdom added: 'They said this of a man's own wife, how much more of his fellow's wife! Hence the sages have said: "He that talks much with womankind brings evil upon himself and neglects the study of the Law and at the last will inherit Gehenna."'[285] These warnings against talking to women reflect the tendency in the Judaism of Jesus' day to exclude women from public life. This exclusion of women from public life went so far in Jerusalem that the upper-class, pious virgins 'were accustomed to stay within the house before marriage as far as possible'; while 'married women left it only with their faces covered'.[286] Such seclusion of women is not found in the Old Testament.

In religious affairs too there operated a tendency to exclude women:

> Women were allowed admittance to the courtyard of the temple only up to a certain limit (the 'Court of Women'), they could offer no sacrifice, they did not count when it was being determined whether the quorum of worshippers necessary for a synagogue service was present, and in the synagogues they were kept separate from men.[287]

Legally women were disadvantaged in various ways. They were not allowed to give evidence in court.[288] As in Old Testament times, polygamy was permitted, and that devalued wives. According to the Hillelites (the rabbinic school which followed Rabbi Hillel) a man could divorce his wife for burning his food or if he met a prettier woman.[289] This liberal outlook of the Hillelites established itself throughout Palestine and the diaspora.[290] That this left wives at the mercy of their husband's caprice and power is very obvious. To sum up. In the Judaism of Jesus' time the woman was valued less highly than the man in religion, law and in morality. This devaluation led to her religious and social oppression, indeed often to her being despised by men.

Despite the indubitable oppression and disadvantage of women in Judaism at the time of Jesus, we must beware of overpressing the trend towards discrimination. In contrast to Roman and Greek attitudes, the Jews had not grown tired of marriage.[291] Marriage was regarded as a duty from which no one was exempt.[292] So, for example, Rabbi Eliezer ben Hyrcanus said: 'Whoever does not practise procreation is like someone who sheds blood.'[293] The maintenance of the institution of marriage, which in Judaism was overwhelmingly monogamous, was an important protection for women. With this value placed on marriage went an explicitly high status of the woman as a wife and a widespread honouring of her as mother.[294] The rabbis often exhort the man to love and honour his wife, because 'the wife is her husband's good fortune, his life, his wealth and his crown'.[295] But the rabbis' positive remarks all relate to the married woman, not to women in general.[296] 'As a person in her own right the woman is a nobody.'[297] However much at least some of the rabbis praise wives and mothers, they do little to recognize that the woman has value in her own right if she is not actually a wife or mother.

Jesus' behaviour is free from the disdain for women that was then widespread in Judaism. He broke quite consciously with Jewish custom when, for example, he had a long discussion with the Samaritan woman (John 4). How extraordinary his behaviour was then is shown by his disciples' reaction: 'They marvelled that he was talking with a woman' (John 4:27). The content of the conversation shows how seriously Jesus took women. Jesus deigns to reveal to this morally disreputable woman (*cf.* vv 17–18) his mission and messiahship (vv. 21–6). Cardinal Faulhaber has aptly described this self-revelation of Jesus to a woman as 'the religious coming of age of the female sex'.[298] Jesus also let it be known that women were equal to men in God's eyes. In contrast to the practice of Jewish teachers of the law[299] he had women among his followers, who were able to share in his teaching, preaching, and extraordinary deeds. Jesus welcomed it when, like his disciples, women joined in being instructed by him (Luke 10:38–42). His proclamation did not put one sex at an advantage over the other, but it was valid for all without reserve: 'Come to me, *all* who labour and are heavy laden, and I will give you rest. Take my yoke upon you, and learn from me . . .' (Matt 11:28). Jesus' parables contain many striking examples drawn from the world of women (*cf.* Matt 13:33; 24:41; Luke 15:8–10; 18:1–8; Mark 12:41–4). 'This distinguished them from rabbinic parables and miracle stories . . . in which women seldom are spoken of, and then more often in a bad sense.'[300]

The proclamation of Jesus is completely free from every form of open or concealed disdain for women, such as frequently characterises rabbinic tradition. For example, Jesus breaks with the morally elevated status of men in the Judaism of his time: instead of warning like the rabbis of the danger of men being seduced by women, he warns against the male tendency to seduce women (Matt 5:27–30). He thereby eliminates any basis for the rabbinic tendency to see women as morally less than equal to men. Instead of warning about the dangers of women, he emphasises the wickedness of the *human* heart, which affects both sexes equally.

Jesus does not just address the moral superiority of men in the Judaism of his day (Matt 5:27–30), but also their legal superiority. In Mark 10:2–12 he condemns every kind of divorce, despite the Old Testament permission of divorce, and thereby protects women from capricious discharge by their husbands. For both sexes he underlines the indissolubility of marriage as the valid will of God. In this passage he makes it clear that polygamy does not fit in with his view of marriage; this is based entirely on Genesis 2:24, which speaks of *one* husband and *one* wife. By his demand for indissoluble monogamy he protects the woman from the devaluation that was inevitably bound up with Jewish divorce practice and legalised polygamy. Marianne Weber correctly writes that Jesus' demand for strict monogamy for husbands as well introduced 'a revolution in the relationship between the sexes'.[301] In committing *both* sexes to life-long fidelity without the possibility of divorce, Jesus opposed all the legal arrangements of the ancient world which permitted husbands much more liberty with regard to the marriage bond than it permitted women![302]

Jesus shows no trace of the tendency in contemporary Judaism to value men more highly from a religious standpoint. Women are just as much called to submit to God's rule and threatened by divine judgement as men (*cf.* Matt 11:28–9). Jesus' proclamation is addressed to all people, and therefore equally to women and to men. Through his absolute love command (Matt 7:12; 22:34–40 and parallels) he throws out once and for all every kind of male egoism or oppression of women. With this demand, and by making possible love and selflessness, Jesus shows the only way in which the relationship between the sexes, a relationship that has been upset by sin, can be healed. And Jesus himself lived out in exemplary fashion the selfless love which he demanded.

His compassionate and healing love – not mere theories about the equality of the sexes – is the fundamental basis for his unique relationship to women. Jesus did not just take women seriously as people who have the same value as men, but in an unprecedented way he turned his attention to suffering and morally despised women. Women as well as men could experience Jesus' healing power (*cf.* Mark 1:29–31; 5:25–34; Matt 9:18, 23–5; 15:21–8; Luke 8:2; 13:10–17). Jesus even set aside the Jewish sabbath regulations in order to heal a hunch-backed woman during a synagogue service (Luke 13:10–17). Answering the objections of the synagogue president, he described the healed woman as a 'daughter of Abraham', an honorific description which is never found in the Talmud.[303] Jesus adopts a protective attitude towards morally despised women without denying their sinfulness (*cf.* Luke 7:36–50; John 7:53–8:11). In controversy with national religious leaders he is not scared of the scandalous word of judgement: 'Truly, I say to you, the tax collectors and the harlots go into the kingdom of God before you' (Matt 21:31). In his teaching Jesus is also not afraid of pointing to women as spiritual examples. He praises the faith of the widow who places all her money in the temple collecting box (Mark 12:41–4 and parallels), he is amazed by the faith of the Syrophoenician woman (Matt 15:21–8 and parallels), he praises the queen of Sheba's quest for truth (Matt 12:41–2 and parallels), and he sets up the importunate widow as an example for his disciples (Luke 18:1–8). It is not surprising that women reacted to Jesus' attention with great trust and love. And so Jesus had to protect women time and again against men's lack of understanding. He defended against the attacks of his disciples the woman who anointed his head with precious oil (Matt 26:6–13 and parallels). He backed up the woman of ill-repute (perhaps a prostitute) who out of gratitude anointed his feet with myrrh, even though he thereby incurred the wrath of his host (Luke 7:36–50). He corrected his disciples when they harshly discouraged the women who wanted to bring their children to Jesus (Matt 19:13–15 and parallels).[304]

He allowed women healed by him to join his band of followers (Luke 8:1–2), and gladly accepted the hospitality (Luke 10:38–42) and the assistance of women (Luke 8:3; Matt 27:55). Jesus' unique attention to women was met by them with responsive love and support, which put the disciples to shame. Whereas the disciples all fled when he was arrested (Matt 26:56 and parallels), and at his crucifixion only John was present (John 19:26–7), several women among his followers were nearby or within sight during his final hours (Matt 27:55 and parallels; John 19:25).[305] The faithfulness of these women continued after his death. They rose on the first Easter morning to anoint his body (Matt 28:1 and parallels) and so were honoured to be the first witnesses of the resurrection (*cf.* Matt 28:9–10; John 20:1–8). In this way not just the earthly Jesus Christ, but the resurrected Christ demonstrated with mighty power that with his coming a new age for women had broken in. In Jesus God's valuation of woman as man's equal companion appears with total clarity, and finally makes obsolete the tendency still present in the Old Testament to regard women as of lesser worth.

3   The Distinction Between the Sexes

If Jesus, unconcerned by the opinion of his contemporaries, decisively proclaimed by word and deed the equality of the sexes, he just as firmly maintained the distinction between them. The gospels leave no doubt that Jesus presupposed a different approach and a distinctive role for men and women. A notable proof of this is his own activity which recognises a quite different commission for the sexes in the service of God. It is striking that Jesus called only men into the circle of the twelve apostles. That is also true for the mission of the seventy (Luke 10:1–16). At the Last Supper only the apostles could have been present (*cf.* Matt 26:17–20 and parallels), although several women from his band of followers, including his own mother, were present in Jerusalem.[306]

If one accepts that according to the synoptic gospels Jesus' last supper was a passover meal (*cf.* Matt 26:17–19 and parallels; Luke 22:15), at which women and children normally participated, the fact that Jesus restricted participation to the twelve apostles is even more striking. Since Jesus was on this occasion instituting the celebration of the Lord's Supper as a regular act of church worship (*cf.* Luke 22:19; 1 Cor 11:23–6) the conclusion of the Swedish exegete B. Gärtner is obvious: 'This demarcation at the Last Supper must have a quite defined meaning, namely that the apostles should deal with the mystery that was committed to them during the meal.'[307] Jesus' call of men alone and his behaviour at the Last Supper go together: Jesus publicly committed the spiritual leadership of his community to men. This fits in with what he did after the resurrection: he conferred the task of worldwide evangelisation and instruction on men (*i.e.*, the disciples; see Matt 28:16–20; Mark 16:14–15; John 20:21–3).

That Jesus only called men to be apostles cannot be dismissed as mere chance or thoughtless accommodation to the one-sided male attitudes of his time. The call of the disciples was rather a quite conscious and considered act. Mark 3:13 says explicitly that Jesus called 'those he wanted' (NIV). Luke 6:12 reports that this call was the fruit of a night of prayer by himself. Jesus' decision to call only men as apostles was, then, the result of an intensive spiritual testing in prayer.

The Vatican declaration *Inter insigniores* is therefore to be agreed with. When Jesus called no women into the circle of the twelve 'he did not do this to fit in with the habits of his time, for his treatment of women is uniquely different from his environment and represents a deliberate and courageous break with it'.[308] The French New Testament scholar Albert Descamps rightly says that 'Jesus possessed the necessary freedom to have dared to entrust the proclamation of the kingdom of God to women, if he had wanted to and believed that this was part of God's plan'.[309] Obviously Jesus proceeded on the assumption that God wanted to entrust the leadership of his community to men.

It is not difficult to see that here Jesus thought and acted completely in accord with Genesis 2, where too the man is entrusted with the task of spiritual leadership.[310] In fact the gospels make it clear that Jesus recognized Genesis 1 and 2 as a valid revelation of God's creative will and he presupposed it in his preaching. In Matthew 19:4ff. (and parallels), on the subject of divorce, against the law of Deuteronomy 24:1 he appeals to Genesis 1 and 2 as the original creation ordinance, which should now be put into practice, since God's kingdom has broken in with his coming.[311] Jesus' preaching is therefore intended to realise the original will of the creator as it is expressed in Genesis 1 and 2. Against this background it is self-evident that Jesus could not have called any women as apostles, for this would have contradicted God's creation ordinance: 'God created woman as man's helper. That forms the basis of the relationship between the sexes. To the man is ascribed the role of leader, to the woman that of supporting and helping the man. Jesus does not need to emphasise this, as it had long been familiar to the Israelite communities.'[312] It is therefore not surprising that Jesus does not express himself more fully about the relationship between, and the different tasks of, the sexes. He presupposes in his thought and acts Genesis 1 and 2 as authoritative divine revelation.

This is shown not just by his exclusively calling men to apostleship, but by the service rendered by women who belonged to Jesus' band of followers. Luke 8:2–3 mentions women who provided for the circle of disciples 'out of their means'. The Greek word for 'provide' is in the imperfect tense, which points to a regular task of the women. It describes 'the quite personal service rendered to another person', which covers both waiting at table and also generally providing support.[313] The women among Jesus' followers saw themselves as 'helpmeets' in the sense of Genesis 2:18, helpmeets of Jesus and his disciples. There is not a single passage in the gospels which points to women who followed Jesus being entrusted with the task of preaching. In this regard it may be noted that even Luke's gospel, with its bias towards women, restricts the title 'disciple' exclusively to Jesus' male disciples,[314] though the call to discipleship is valid for both sexes. The women who followed Jesus are also conceptually distinguished from the circle of disciples. In distinction from the disciples, they were clearly not called in a special way: 'The basis of their service [according to Luke 8:2] depended much more on their healing from demons and sickness.'[315] In sum, we see that Jesus did not just express the equality of the sexes in word and action, but that he also respected the individuality of male and female in the sense of Genesis 2. Certainly the women in Jesus' circle did not feel that their exclusion from the apostleship and preaching was discriminatory, 'for they were happy in the certainty that the Redeemer regarded them as men's equal'.[316]

Jesus did not just see men as the carriers of his movement: the man was 'head' also in the realm of nature. One indication of this is that Jesus retained traditional Jewish phraseology about marriage. He speaks in the active voice of the man 'marrying' (*gamizein*), but uses the passive 'being married' (*gamizesthai*) for the woman.[317] This way of speaking is quite compatible with the sense of Genesis 2:24, for there too the active is used for the man's role in marriage. He takes the initiative and makes the decision about marital union, for it is he who leaves his parents and enters the bond with his wife:

'Therefore a man leaves his father and mother and cleaves to his wife, and they become one flesh.' How seriously Jesus takes the man's special responsibility emerges from Matthew 5:27–30. Instead of pointing, like contemporary Jews did, to woman as the dangerous seducer, Jesus warns of the danger of seduction sponsored by the man: 'I say to you that every one who looks at a married woman so that she becomes lustful, has already caused her to commit adultery in her heart' (v. 28).[318]

The New Testament scholar Klaus Haacker has adduced serious philological and contextual reasons for holding that what is meant here is not the spontaneous lustful glance, but the demanding look that leads the woman to adulterous desires.[319] However, the most striking point about this passage is that Jesus addresses the man as the one particularly responsible for relations between the sexes, and he does not allow the male excuse that they are seduced by women.

The great exegete Karl Bornhäuser must be thanked for bringing out this aspect of Jesus' words. He aptly paraphrases Jesus' teaching: 'Relations between you and women must be pure and remain pure . . . *You, men*, have the duty of bringing this about. The purification and healing of relations between the sexes must begin with you.'[320] In calling men to fulfil their special responsibilities in the spiritual and natural realms, Jesus confirms indirectly the position of the man expressed in Genesis 2 as 'head' of the woman. At the same time he attacks every degeneration of male leadership into chauvinist despotism, as he removes the Old Testament and Jewish right of a man to divorce his wife. Arbitrary male rule of women is abolished by Jesus, in that he binds both sexes to unconditional mutual love and devotion to God, and promises the necessary power to carry it out. God's rule spells the end of all egotistically perverted rule of women by men. In God's new kingdom, initiated by Jesus, there is still both authority and subordination, the man leads and the woman is led. But in place of arbitrary male domination there is a reign of love, a humble leadership which is to be seen entirely as service given to the wife (*cf.* Mark 9:35).

7

Man and Woman in Paul's Teaching

1 The Affirmation of Sexuality

The apostle Paul[321] is the biblical writer most often charged
with attitudes opposing the body and sexuality.[322] More
careful study of his epistles leads to a different conclusion.
There is not a single remark of Paul's that treats the body as
such or its sexuality as despicable or of little value.

Paul's attitude to the body and to sex must be understood
entirely against the background of his thinking about creation. His attitude is formulated most pregnantly in 1 Timothy
4:4: '. . . Everything created by God is good.' This fundamental 'yes' to creation determines the apostle's attitude to food
offered to idols in Romans 14, where he emphasises that
'nothing is unclean in itself' (Rom 14:14); his stand against the
ascetic tendencies in the church at Colossae (Col 2:16ff.); and
his attitude towards the bodily and the sexual. The Pauline
understanding of Christian freedom is also intelligible only
when it is viewed against the background of his unlimited
affirmation of the creation. In 1 Corinthians 3:22–3 Paul calls
out that the cosmos (v. 22) is at the Christian's disposal: '. . .
All are yours; and you are Christ's; and Christ is God's.' The
believer possesses the freedom to use for God's service and
for his glorification all that God has created.

In view of this unconditional affirmation of the creation it is
natural that Paul also affirms without restriction the body and
its sexuality. In 1 Corinthians 6:19–20 he even describes the
body of the believer as the temple of the Holy Spirit (v. 19),

which should serve to glorify God (v. 20). It is hardly possible to put a higher valuation on the human body. Man's body is not, as in many other religions, something to be contended with or that is opposed to God. It is appointed to be the dwelling of the living God. How far removed is this high valuation of the body from the Platonic view, which sees the body only as the prison of the soul! Paul therefore could not have supported any spiritualising antipathy to the body, because he knew that in Jesus Christ God himself had appeared in bodily form (*cf*. Rom 1:3; 8:3; 9:5; Phil 2:7; Eph 2:14–15; Col 1:22; 1 Tim 3:16).

Paul was just as far from divinising the body as regarding it as demonic. He knew that the body can become a source of danger because of human sinfulness. But that does not call in question its character as God's good creation. It is in this sense that all those passages are to be understood in which Paul expresses a close connection between the body and man being a sinner (*cf*. Rom 6:6; 7:18–23; Gal 5:24). Paul knew that only when the body obeyed God did it serve to glorify God; otherwise it became an instrument of sin. Therefore he urged: 'present your bodies as a living sacrifice, holy and acceptable to God' (Rom 12:1). Only through faith and obedience does the body cease to be an instrument of sin and become a temple of the Holy Spirit (1 Cor 6:19). That is not to say that the body as such is sinful, if the person does not believe in Jesus. Rather the body is a good creation of God that is set either in a sinful or in a God-pleasing direction. It is therefore a serious misunderstanding if, from those passages where Paul describes the connection of the body with sin, it is concluded that the apostle is in principle against the body. Paul rather wants the body to fulfil its divinely intended role.

From this standpoint we must understand those passages where Paul seems to speak negatively about the body, of pommelling it and subduing it (1 Cor 9:27) to gain an imperishable crown. The apostle wants to express here in vivid imagery that his body must be totally at the disposal of God's goals and purposes. The body must not stand in the way of the fulfilment of God's will, even when this involves painful self-denial or physical suffering. This passage can only be rightly understood when it is read as Paul's personal testimony; he had been prepared to endure the most severe physical suffering because of his call to be the apostle to the Gentiles (*cf.* 2 Cor 6:3–10; 12:10; Acts 14:19). In 1 Corinthians 9:27 Paul shows through his example the obligation that is imposed on all Christians to make their bodies entirely available for God's service. How much physical suffering arises out of such dedication to God differs from believer to believer. At any rate it is apparent that 1 Corinthians 9:27 cannot be cited in proof of Paul's alleged hostility to the body.

From this positive attitude to the body a positive attitude to sex and sexuality necessarily follows. The most striking testimony to Paul's 'yes' to sexuality is found in 1 Corinthians 7. This chapter disproves all theories which ascribe to Paul a contempt for sexuality. In 1 Corinthians 7:3–5 Paul *obliges* both spouses to be ready at any time for marital intercourse. In this passage Paul consciously rejects the ascetic tendencies in Corinth, which obviously arose out of a devaluation of sex. On the contrary Paul insists that sexual relations within marriage are not just a possibility, which can be set aside by either side, but a duty based on love.

Sexual abstinence within marriage is then only spiritually justified if it is for a limited period and agreed between both parties.[323] This is because for Paul sex is a gift of God which cannot be abjured without punishment. In verse 9 he warns explicitly against a self-imposed celibacy which overrates one's own capacity for abstinence. A life-long renunciation of marriage and sex is therefore not commanded by him, but is a gift of grace (v. 7) given to one, but not to another. Marriage is also according to Paul a gift (v. 7), not a necessary evil, as is often imputed to him. The assessment of marriage as a gift is proof of the high value Paul placed on marriage, human sexuality, and sex.

There are exegetes[324] who see a devaluation of marriage and sex precisely in 1 Corinthians 7, because here Paul apparently rates celibacy more highly than marriage. Without going into all the detailed issues, we want at least to sketch the outlines of Paul's attitude to marriage and celibacy in 1 Corinthians 7.

Excursus 4
The relationship of marriage and celibacy in 1 Corinthians 7

Two facts, which have not always been noted, are decisive in the interpretation of this chapter.

1. Paul is replying to questions raised by the Corinthians in a letter to him (v. 1). He is not therefore expounding a systematic theology of marriage and celibacy which takes account of all relevant points of view. It is rather a statement by Paul, prompted by the situation, with various omissions which he fills out elsewhere (*cf.* Eph 5:22ff.) So, for example, whoever concludes from verse 9 ('if they cannot exercise self-control, they should marry') that Paul regards marriage only as a necessary outlet for sexual desire and is not concerned with the intellectual and psychological dimension, overlooks the fact that the chapter is addressing a particular situation. This is also to forget that Paul can speak of the symbolic-spiritual significance of the marriage bond in a way that leaves everything he has said before about marriage far behind (Eph 5:22 ff.).

2. 1 Corinthians 7 is a mixture of *binding instruction*, in which Paul appeals partially to Jesus himself (vv. 10–11), and *personal opinion*, which he tries to make understood (vv. 12, 25–6, 40) but which he imposes on no one. Any interpretation which ignores these points will come to seriously mistaken conclusions.

So we want to sum up in a series of points what 1 Corinthians 7 teaches about marriage and celibacy, to clarify whether Paul really disparages marriage and sex.

1. According to verse 7 Christian marriage and also celibacy for God's sake is a charism (*i.e.*, a gift of divine grace) whose reception cannot be compelled. Characterising marriage as a charism protects it once and for all from disparagement.

2. According to verse 14 marriage secures the 'sanctification' of an unbelieving partner by the Christian spouse. If Paul had viewed marriage only as a necessary device to tame human sexual needs, it could not effect the sanctification of a non-Christian partner. The

sanctifying effect of a Christian marriage mentioned here flows from its character as a gift of grace. Christian marriage for Paul is a bond created by God in which God's grace is realised in a special way, grace which even includes an unbelieving partner.

3. Paul presupposes marriage as the normal vocation of a Christian. In verse 2 he writes that because of the temptation to immorality each one should be married. The expression 'each one' should not be pressed too hard, but it does show that for Paul marriage is the normal lifestyle for Christians.

4. Paul tends to recommend celibacy as the better lifestyle for those who are still single. This is because of eschatological pressures and to enable them to be more available for God (vv. 26–40). But in this regard certain points must be noted.

a. Paul characterises his attitude as personal *advice* (vv. 25–6, 40) and shows understanding if it is not followed (vv. 28, 36, 38).

b. Paul allows the Corinthians complete freedom (vv. 28, 36, 38), and indeed warns lest his own advice be regarded as restraint.

c. Paul never goes back on his remark that the renunciation of marriage is a gift of grace, which can be demanded of no one (v. 9). He does not speak in favour of self-chosen celibacy, but accepts only that renunciation of marriage where God gives the grace to will it and carry it through.

d. Paul sometimes employs the expression that those who are still single should not strive or seek (*zēteo*) for marriage. This is not to say that when Christians recognise God's guidance to marry those concerned should prefer to remain single. Paul was convinced that ultimately it depends on God's will and grace whether a Christian is destined to celibacy or marriage. Adolf Schlatter aptly remarks in his commentary on 1 Corinthians 7. 'But because the state of celibacy presupposes divinely given grace, he [Paul] cannot demand it. Law and grace must not be confused. Grace works freely.'[325] On the grace of celibacy Schlatter remarks: 'Whoever has it, is bound to it as a sacred duty. But it binds no one except those who receive it.'[326]

For our study the decisive point is that Paul's motive for recommending the celibate state is not asceticism or hostility to the body, but is spiritual. Paul recommends celibacy for God's sake, in order that the Christian may be more fully available for God's service (vv. 32–5) in view of the eschatological pressures. Paul does not recommend celibacy because he rejects, despises, or undervalues marriage and sex.

We can therefore conclude this section as follows. Paul affirms (as does Jesus in Matt 19:4–6) the value of creation and consequently the value of the body and sex. But for God's sake sexuality (as with Jesus in Matt 19:11–12) is relativised. That this relativisation of sexuality does not mean its abolition is apparent from all those passages where Paul even in spiritual matters (*e.g.*, in church life) takes account of the sexually determined character of both married and unmarried believers. The theory of a Paul who is hostile to the body thus founders on the Pauline texts.

2   The Equality of the Sexes

Paul has not merely been charged with hostility to the body, but again and again with hostility towards women. Through his devaluation of women, so it is said, he came into contradiction with Jesus, who in word and deed opposed every kind of devaluation of women. Whereas Jesus is supposed to have broken with the patriarchal ideas of his time, Paul fell back into Jewish attitudes which degraded women. A careful study of the Pauline letters shows, however, that this view is untenable. The apostle makes it clear many times that he upholds the equality of women as Jesus did. Paul expresses his convictions about the inherent equality of the sexes in sublime fashion when he writes in Galatians 3:27–8: 'For as many of you as were baptized into Christ have put on Christ. There is neither Jew nor Greek, there is neither slave nor free, there is neither male nor female; for you are all one in Christ Jesus.'

This passage shows that in the church of Jesus there is no difference in value between different social classes, and different sexes. Since all constitute a single unity in Christ Jesus the superiority of Jews over Gentiles, freemen over slaves, or men over women, has no justification in the light of Christ's revelation. Paul is in no way saying that all these differences are simply extinguished or have no further significance for the shape of church life. For it is obvious to

Paul that national, social, and sexual differences continue even among Christians. Paul did not preach about the levelling out of natural and social differences. He did not try to prevent Jewish Christians from keeping the law or demand that Gentile Christians should keep the Mosaic law. He did not demand the abolition of slavery among Christians (see Philm), and he consistently recognised the differentiation of the sexes in the shaping of church life (*cf.* 1 Cor 11, 14). Yet he emphasised in Galatians 3:28 the complete parity of all believers 'in Christ'. How is this apparent discrepancy to be understood? That on the one hand Paul allows these differences a significance within the church of Jesus, and on the other affirms their abolition 'in Christ'? Some commentators have wanted to see a contradiction within Paul's teaching, claiming that he has not drawn out all the necessary consequences of the understanding he had arrived at in Galatians 3:28.[327]

The interpretation of this passage depends completely on how the formula 'in Christ' is to be understood. The expression 'in Christ' is found quite frequently in Paul's epistles and means the new life that is given to those who believe in Christ. 'If any one is in Christ, he is a new creation' (2 Cor 5:17). 'In Christ' people are saved from being lost (2 Tim 2:10); they receive forgiveness of sins (Eph 4:32; Rom 8:1), free access to God (Eph 3:12), rebirth (1 Cor 15:22; 2 Cor 5:17; Eph 2:10,13), resurrection from the dead (1 Cor 15:22; 1 Thess 4:16), and eternal life (Rom 6:23; 2 Tim 1:1). But the expression 'in Christ' does not just describe the new existence in which the individual Christian personally participates, but the new existence of the whole church of Jesus. 'We, though many, are one body in Christ' (Rom 12:5). All this shows that the formula 'in Christ' describes the church's objective state of salvation.[328] Galatians 3:28 means, therefore, that *as far as eternal salvation is concerned*, all, *whether male or female*, are equal before God and that each one may enjoy divine sonship through faith in Jesus (*cf.* Gal 3:29). Paul is here in complete agreement with Jesus, who unconditionally offered a share in the kingdom of God to both sexes. The religious equality of men and women, as represented by Paul and Jesus, does not permit one sex to regard itself as superior to the other. However, the identical position of the sexes as regards salvation does not of course mean that for Jesus or Paul the specific character of the sexes is irrelevant for building the kingdom of God or the church. When Galatians 3:28 says that Jews and Greeks, men and women, are all 'one in Christ', it is talking about the fundamental unity which comprises all believers and consists of the common union of all with Christ. But it does not involve a homogeneity in which the created differences of people, including their sexuality, are levelled out. Paul made it clear once and for all in 1 Corinthians 12, with the picture of the body of Christ, that the church of Jesus represents a unity, but that this unity comprises various members with different tasks. There is therefore no contradiction when in Galatians 3:28 Paul on the one hand attests the abolition of all created human differences *before God* (that is in respect of salvation) and on the other emphasises the continuing significance of created differences for *living together as people* in the church of Christ. Paul thus recognises the complete equality of men and women (Gal 3:28) without denying that the sexes were created to be different.

The equality of men and women expressed in Galatians 3:28 governs all Paul's thought. The apostle never differentiates between the sexes when it concerns questions of faith, salvation, or ethical standards. The offer and the demands of the gospel apply equally to men and women. A good example of the equality of the sexes in Paul's teaching is 1 Corinthians 7, where like Jesus he forbids *both* sexes to divorce (vv. 10–13) and allows the wife the same right to sexual union as the husband (vv. 1–5). He also indicates that the unbelieving partner is 'sanctified' by the wife or by the husband (v. 14). Through these observations it becomes clear how Paul really regards the wife as an inherently equal partner, who has the same right to loving devotion as the husband.

Paul's convictions about the equality of the sexes also governed his relations with people. His behaviour is completely free of any devaluation of women.[329] One piece of evidence is the list of greetings at the end of Romans (Rom 16:3–15): the first of the twenty-eight people he greets is a woman (v. 3), Prisca (also called Priscilla), who with her husband the Jewish tentmaker Aquila was one of the apostle's closest friends. That Paul, like Luke who is also very sympathetic to women, mentions Prisca before her husband shows the special regard in which he held this woman. He praises her and her husband because they saved his life at the risk of their own. In verse 12 Paul greets the 'beloved Persis, who has worked hard in the Lord'. This remark again shows Paul's high regard for women who lead exemplary Christian lives. The social position of women does not matter to him. It is very possible that 'beloved Persis' was a slave, since 'Persis is a typical name for a slave'.[330] In the next verse Paul extols the mother of Rufus, who has also become his mother because 'she received him with real motherly love and care'.[331] In 2 Timothy 1:5 Paul reminds his co-worker Timothy of the exemplary faith of his mother and grandmother (cf. 2 Tim 3:15). In his other letters Paul greets women (Philm 2) or singles them out for praise (Phil 4:2–3; 2 Tim 4:19).

How seriously Paul took women is shown by the fact that he allowed a woman to divert him at least temporarily from his spiritual principle of supporting himself by working (cf. 1 Cor 9:1–18; 1 Thess 2:9; 2 Thess 3:8; Acts 18:3; 20:33–5). Lydia, a seller of purple, succeeded in persuading the apostle to make an exception to his usual practice (cf. Acts 16:15; Phil 4:10–18; 2 Cor 11:9).[332]

All these passages show that Paul upheld in practice the equality of men and women which he preached in his epistles. There is no trace of hostility to women either in his letters or in the apostle's life.

3   The Distinction Between the Sexes

The apostle Paul is not merely aware of the equality of the sexes but also of their different places and functions. Fun-

damental for his view of the relationship of men and women is
1 Corinthians 11:3: 'I want you to realise that the head of
every man is Christ, and the head of the woman is man, and
the head of Christ is God' (NIV). Paul speaks here of four
levels: God – Christ – man – woman. The Greek term *kephalē*
(head) expresses a relationship of subordination. 'It means
that the one who stands over the other conceptually is the
basis of the other's existence.'[333] So as Christ comes from the
Father, is subordinate to the Father and lives for him, so the
woman lives 'in a way appropriate to her existence from the
man and for the man's sake'[334] as a companion subordinate to
him (*cf.* 1 Cor 11:8–9). The fourfold order of levels reappears
again and again in Paul: both Jesus' subordination to the
Father (*cf.* Phil 2:8; Rom 5:19; 1 Cor 15:26–8) and the
woman's subordination to the man (Eph 5:22ff.; Col 3:18; Tit
2:5) are mentioned several times. It is worth noting that Paul
in 1 Corinthians 11:3 compares woman's subordination to
man with the subordination of Jesus Christ to God the Father.

This comparison makes it clear that the subordination of
woman to man envisaged by Paul has nothing to do with
devaluing or oppressing women. It shows rather that super-
or subordination of persons of equal worth is intended. For it
would be absurd to conclude from the subordination of Christ
to the Father that Christ was of less value than God the
Father, for the apostle was convinced that Christ was God
without reserve (*cf.* Rom 9:5; 2 Cor 12:8; Phil 2:6–7; Col
1:15ff; 2:2–3, 9–10; Tit 2:13).[335] To that extent 1 Corinthians
11:3 disproves the claim that by emphasising the primacy of
the man Paul had undercut the equality of the sexes he
expressed in Galatians 3:28. Paul saw rather in the example of
the Trinity that equality is not opposed to super- or subordination. At the same time the Trinity clarifies in what way the
man's divinely intended primacy should be exercised and in
what way not. Since his headship has its model in the headship
of God the Father over Jesus Christ, this removes any
justification for a man to rule his wife despotically. As God's
lordship over the Son is a reign of unconditional love seeking
the Son's best, so man's leadership must be a reign of selfless

love which is concerned solely with the woman's well-being. The woman is not intended to be merely receptive in this relationship. She is to consent to the leadership and love of the man, for in the relationship between Christ and the Father the mutuality of love and the total *union* in fellowship is visible in incomparable beauty. So too the relationship between man and woman is governed not just by super- and subordination, but through mutual loving and being loved, through becoming one flesh in total communion.

It is patently obvious that the relationship between man and wife can only be a very pale reflection of the love of God. But that the sexes are deemed worthy to portray on earth the glory of the inner life of God is a most striking proof of man's uniquely high status among the creatures. It is not just the individual person who is an image of God, but the fellowship between man and wife is an image of God, since both together reflect the trinitarian fellowship of love. All this shows that the woman's subordination to the man has nothing to do with any kind of contempt for women. Werner Meyer writes in his commentary on Corinthians: 'In the loving submission of the woman to the man is reflected the inner trinitarian glory of the relationship of the Son to the Father. Could anything greater be said about women?'[336]

Paul's conviction about male headship expressed in 1 Corinthians 11:3 governs his thinking about the place and function of the sexes in the church and also in marriage. We now want to examine Paul's outlook in both areas in turn.

4   Man and Woman in the Church

Whenever Paul discusses the differing position of the sexes in the church he always has one end in view: he wants the divinely intended position of the man as head of the woman to be expressed throughout church life. He also insists that the differences between the sexes should not be obliterated. It is against this background that Paul's much-misunderstood remarks about the position of women in the church are to be understood.

One of these controversial texts is 1 Corinthians 11:3–16. Here Paul demands that the women wear a head-covering[337] when they pray and prophesy, whereas men should pray with their heads uncovered. It may seem unintelligible to the modern reader why Paul should lay so much weight on an apparently trivial external. We shall give a few important indications as to how it should be understood, without being able to discuss all the exegetical details.

1. The key to a deeper understanding of this text is found in the opening verse of the section: 'I want you to realise that the head of every man is Christ, and the head of the woman is man, and the head of Christ is God' (v. 3, NIV). Paul is concerned that the position of the man as head of the wife, and the wife as subordinate helpmeet of the man (*cf.* v. 9), should be outwardly expressed in the church. The custom generally current in the Christian church at that period, of women covering their heads, served to symbolise the divinely intended primacy of the man. Paul is fundamentally misunderstood when he is imputed as clinging narrow-mindedly to an existing custom. The custom of covering the head is important for him only because it expresses his non-negotiable conviction of the man's divinely intended headship. The apostle is not in the first place fighting for a custom but for the observance of the relationship between the sexes appointed by God. The Corinthian women, in laying aside their headgear, were rebelling against their divinely intended subordination and proclaiming an equality with men that contradicted the order of creation. The church father Chrysostom (345–407) wrote of the behaviour of the Corinthian women: 'Do not tell me it is a trivial fault, it is disobedience. And if the matter were small in itself, it would have become important because it was a symbol of something great.'[338]

Thus Paul's apparently petty fight about the women's headgear is fundamentally a most important theological battle, both against the desire to obliterate gender differences and against the Corinthian women's rebellion against the position given to woman at creation.

2. It is therefore misguided to conclude from the culturally conditioned custom of the headgear that the whole section 1 Corinthians 11:3–16 is culturally conditioned and therefore obsolete for us. Paul is defending in this passage eternally valid truths of revelation (the hierarchical order within the Trinity and between the sexes) which are apparent not just in Genesis 2 (*cf.* the primacy of the man in Gen 2:18) but also in Christ (*cf.* the subordination of Christ to the Father, Matt 26:39, 42 and parallels; John 4:34; 6:38, and the primacy of men maintained by Jesus calling exclusively male apostles). Whether the primitive Christian custom of covering the head which Paul defended is still binding today is another question. Certainly our situation, when it comes to headgear, is fundamentally different from the situation then. It cannot be said nowadays that the custom of women covering their heads to pray is a custom of the churches of God (v. 16), that is the practice of all Christendom.

The Corinthian women, on the other hand, unilaterally and for spiritually questionable motives, set aside a general custom of the Christian churches of those days. Paul was therefore quite right to oppose it. Since customs change with time, and even in the early church the custom of covering the head was not universal,[339] our situation is quite different. If a Christian woman does not cover her head during public prayer, that does not show (in contrast to the situation then) that she is rebelling against the order of creation. If, however, Christian women think that they should follow Paul's instruction about covering the head, they should not be made fun of, but respected for their stand.

3. When it is recognised that Paul in 1 Corinthians 11 is concerned about maintaining the order of creation of men and women, the difficult verse 10 becomes intelligible: 'That is why [because the woman is created for the man] a woman ought to have a [sign of] authority on her head, because of the angels.' The Greek word *exousia* is understood by some interpreters actively, as 'authority', and by others passively,

as 'power'. However, *exousia* never means 'power' to which one passively submits, but always 'power' which one actively exercises, so 'authority', 'authorisation'.[340] The point of the passage is therefore: if the women pray or prophesy before other members of the church, then they only possess the spiritual authority to do so if they do it obediently, accepting the position assigned to them at creation.[341] For they cannot pray 'in the Spirit' if they rebel against the order of creation hallowed by God's Spirit. This background explains the additional comment 'because of the angels'. The most probable explanation of this rather puzzling comment is that the angels are present when the church prays, and that they keep watch that God's arrangements are kept.[342]

. 4. The text does not intend a degrading subordination of women to men, but honourable behaviour during prayer and prophecy. The Greek word *doxa* in verse 7 is frequently translated 'reflection', although it does not have this meaning in biblical or non-biblical Greek.[343] The correct translation is 'glory'.[344] So as the man is the 'image and glory of God', so the woman is the glory of the man. The woman should behave as befits her glory. This she does if she wears the head-covering that was regarded in Judaism as a sign of her honour.[345] So verses 5 (dishonours the head), 6 (disgraceful), 13 (is it proper?), 14 (degrading) and 15 (pride) show that the whole passage is concerned with preserving womanly honour, and certainly not with demeaning women. The woman upholds her dignity and glory by preserving her womanly character and her position in the creation. Verse 3 also confirms that the passage has nothing to do with demeaning women.

5. It is significant that as regards the subordination of women Paul appeals not to Genesis 3 (the story of the fall) but to Genesis 2 (see 1 Cor 11:9). He thereby shows that male primacy is not a result of the fall, but part of the order of creation (*cf.* v. 3). If the subordination of women were regarded as a consequence of sin, then the head-covering would not be a sign of honour for women, but a shameful sign of her guilt.

To sum up. 1 Corinthians 11:3–16 shows that it was a central concern of Paul to make visible the created subordination of women to men in the Christian church life and to guard against any levelling out of differences between the sexes. This is also the reason why in 1 Corinthians 14:33–8 and 1 Timothy 2:12 he reserves, just as Jesus did, the leadership and instruction of the church exclusively to men. Both these passages, like 1 Corinthians 11, suffer from being misunderstood and being rejected. At least with 1 Corinthians 14:33–8 this is not just due to its content being objectionable to the modern reader, but with genuine difficulties of interpretation within the text.

[33] . . . As in all the churches of the saints, [34]the women should keep silence in the churches. For they are not permitted to speak, but should be subordinate, as even the law says. [35]If there is anything they desire to know, let them ask their husbands at home. For it is shameful for a woman to speak in church. [36]What! Did the word of God originate with you, or are you the only ones it has reached?

[37]If any one thinks that he is a prophet, or spiritual, he should acknowledge that what I am writing to you is a command of the Lord. [38]If any one does not recognise this, he is not recognised.

The chief problem in the interpretation of this text is clarifying how the command to keep silence (1 Cor 14:33ff.) relates to 1 Corinthians 11:3ff., where Paul explicitly allows women to pray and prophesy in church. Is there a contradiction between these two texts, or is the command to keep silent not so absolute as it sounds? Various solutions have been offered, some of which may definitely be ruled out. For example, the suggestion that verses 34–5 do not come from Paul but from a later hand is quite untenable. This solution is disproved by the fact that all manuscripts contain these verses, and only a few insignificant textual witnesses add them to verse 40, which may be adequately explained as a copyist's error. Also to be rejected is the view that 1 Corinthians 14, not 1 Corinthians 11, represents the apostle's real view. This interpretation does not explain at all why in 1 Corinthians 11 Paul so passionately insists that women should cover their heads when praying or prophesying, when he really does not want them to participate in prayer or prophesy at all in church. Only two solutions can in fact be seriously considered.

One solves the apparent tension between 1 Corinthians 11 and 14 by regarding 1 Corinthians 14:34–5 not as an absolute prohibition on speaking but only as a prohibition on teaching, that is participating in a teaching ministry. Women were not forbidden to participate charismatically in the worship, that is to pray and prophesy; they were only prohibited from teaching. In favour of this interpretation it may be pointed out that the terms 'learn' and 'question' in verse 35 suggest a teaching situation, in which authoritative instruction is being given to the church. Further, the parallel passage in 1 Timothy 2:12 speaks explicitly of 'teaching' (*didaskein*) and not at all about speaking.

Although this interpretation is very attractive and illuminating, in my opinion it does not stand up. The wording of verses 34–5 simply rules it out. The Greek term 'to be silent' (*sigaō*) must like the English word be taken in an absolute sense, as a prohibition against any verbal utterance.[346] Verses 28 and 30 show quite clearly that Paul also in 1 Corinthians 14 understands 'being silent' absolutely, as 'not speaking'. The Greek term for speaking (*lalein*) in verse 34 means as in English quite generally 'speak, talk, say'.[347] Its use shows without doubt that Paul does not confine it to 'teaching'. It covers speaking in prayer (vv. 2, 9, 11, 28), prophecy (vv. 3, 6, 29), instruction (vv. 6, 19), words of knowledge (v. 6) and revelation (v. 6). It is therefore impossible in verse 34 suddenly to limit *lalein* to teaching. If Paul had only been forbidding teaching, he would either have used the verb *didaskein* (to teach) or he would have had to add something else as well (as in vv. 6 and 19). Otherwise he could not have used the word 'be silent'. 1 Corinthians 14:34–5 therefore expresses a total ban on women speaking in church worship.

This does not contradict 1 Corinthians 11, where Paul is

dealing with women praying and prophesying in small house groups, whereas in 1 Corinthians 14 he speaks explicitly of the whole church being gathered for worship. Prayer and prophecy did not occur only in public worship. On our passage Schlatter writes: 'Prophecy was not necessarily restricted to the assembled congregation . . . If a woman was commissioned by God to pass on a divine message, she could do so in another way without making a public speech.'[348] Acts 21:10ff. shows that early Christian prophecy was not limited to public worship. It is therefore quite possible that 1 Corinthians 11:3ff. deals with matters pertaining to prayer and prophecy which took place outside worship services, despite the quite general formulation of 1 Corinthians 11:5: 'any woman who prays or prophesies . . .'

What prompts the apostle to insist that women keep silent in divine worship? The reason is the same as in 1 Corinthians 11:3ff.: Paul is concerned that the divinely intended subordination of women to men should be preserved. Paul's command to keep silent has nothing to do with any demeaning of women; he wants rather through this arrangement to preserve the honour and dignity of women, since he is protecting them from unseemly behaviour (1 Cor 14:35).

Charlotte von Kirschbaum, Karl Barth's co-worker, has brought out the positive intention of our text very beautifully. Women should through their ministry of silence

> proclaim that they are submissive. This ministry seems outstandingly important to the apostle: it is a ministry that builds up the church. It would be wrong to see this demand as an unfriendly gesture on the part of the apostle, the silent women represent the listening church, which the teaching church must again and again become. It is the silence of awe before the resurrected one, the Lord of the church. That the women should and can carry out this ministry is connected with the symbolism of their position in nature.[349]

It is similar to 1 Corinthians 11, in that for Paul the demand for silence is not a trivial point of order which he can at his whim impose on the Corinthians, rather it is a most decisive ordinance which to reject is to rebel against God. This is apparent from the grave reasons which he cites in 1 Corinthians 14. He appeals not just to decorum (v. 35) and the practice of the universal church of the time (v. 33), but also to the law (Gen 3:16), and the order of creation which supports it (v. 34), and to a command of the Lord (v. 37).

In Corinthians 14:33ff. Paul does not represent a particular narrow view of the organisation of worship, but he acts as advocate of the universal church against the arbitrariness of the Corinthians. He is fighting, as he has already done in 1 Corinthians 11, that the divinely intended subordination of women to men should remain acknowledged in the Corinthian church. Whoever sets this order aside forfeits, says Paul, God's recognition (v. 38) and with it the church's basis for its existence. In a similar way, according to 1 Corinthians 11:10, women forfeit their right to pray and prophesy if they despise God's created order.

Paul's injunction to silence in 1 Corinthians 14:33ff. is closely associated with his ban on women teaching in 1 Timothy 2:11–12: 'Let a woman learn in silence with all submissiveness. I permit no woman to teach or to have authority over men; she is to keep silent.' The basic idea is once again the same as in 1 Corinthians 11 and 14: it concerns the maintenance of God's created order of male and female. In distinction from 1 Corinthians 14, however, this passage bans only teaching. Paul excludes women from the office of teaching because teaching the assembled congregation would necessarily place them over men. For in contrast to prophecy, which is related to specific situations and according to Paul is subject to assessment by the congregation, teaching is binding and of general validity, so that the congregation must submit to it (cf. Rom 6:17; 16:17; 1 Cor 4:17; 15:15ff.; Col 2:6–7; 2 Thess 2:15). Authorised teaching belongs, as Paul sees it, to the leadership and direction of the congregation and carries with it an obligation on church members to obey it (cf. Eph 4:11; 1 Tim 3:2; 2 Tim 2:24; Tit 1:9).

Because the teacher of the congregation must call for obedience, the office of teacher is not open to a woman according to Paul, as she would otherwise step outside her divinely intended subordination to men. As Schlatter says: 'A woman who taught would give orders to a man, and that Paul does not permit, for she should not rule over men.'[350] If, then, a woman desires the office of teacher or leader, she has, the apostle is convinced, 'deserted God's order and is thereby unfit to bear witness to his will'.[351] 1 Timothy 2:12 shows (just like 1 Cor 14:33ff.) that Paul, exactly like Jesus, entrusted the functions of leadership and direction in the church exclusively to men. 'This involves no downgrading of women, indeed no value judgment at all. It rather defines the areas of their rights and activities in a way which corresponds to the differences in their natural endowments.'[352]

It is interesting that in 1 Timothy 2 Paul cites not just the order of creation (that man was created first and given leadership) as the basis (v. 13), but also 'the greater susceptibility of women to temptation',[353] as hinted at in the story of the fall, which makes her less suited to the office of teacher than a man.[354] But by mentioning Eve's guilt in the fall, Paul does not in any way intend to ascribe to her the main blame. In Romans 5:12 he expressly 'emphasises that despite Eve's previous sin, the misery of sin was first brought upon mankind by Adam . . . It was his sin that was the great disaster for mankind.'[355] So in 1 Timothy 2:14 Paul does not want to charge Eve with the chief responsibility for the fall, only to draw attention to her share of guilt, in which a peculiar danger for women is noticeable, namely their greater susceptibility to temptation. The reference to this particular liability of women shows that in excluding them from the teaching and leadership offices the apostle is not disadvantaging them, but is trying to safeguard their femininity, with its special gifts and weaknesses. Allowing women to teach or lead the congregation would not only offend against God's order of creation, but at the same time open them to risks to which they are not equal. In the story of the fall Paul saw what dangerous consequences are entailed when the woman forsakes her

God-intended position as man's subordinate and helpmeet. Since God's intention that woman should be subordinate is not an oppressive sentence, but a life-saving and protective measure in her own best interests, it must harm her if she rejects this provision. For Paul, to allow a woman to teach or lead is blatantly opposed to her female nature. For this reason, and not for any misogynist motive, he does not permit her to fill such an office in 1 Corinthians 14 or 1 Timothy 2.

Of course this does not mean that women in the early church were condemned to doing nothing. Paul rather 'fully appreciated the effectiveness of women in church service, as long as it corresponded to their female nature and the divine order of creation'.[356] In Romans 16:1f. he commends to the church in Rome his co-worker the deaconess Phoebe.[357] Obviously when the epistle to the Romans was composed there was already an order of deaconesses in the Pauline churches, for the Greek term *diakonos* describes an office.[358] What tasks a deaconess carried out at this time can only be guessed at. It certainly did not involve public proclamation of the word, teaching, or leading the church. Perhaps it involved serving the congregation, by bringing material help to the needy (Rom 16:2),[359] in serving women, the sick, and strangers.[360] We find one clear clue to the duties of a deaconess in 1 Timothy 5:3–16, where Paul discusses the diaconate of those who were enrolled in the order of widows. These widows clearly had the task of serving the congregation, through intensive intercession (*cf.* v. 5) and visiting from house to house (*cf.* v. 13). Paul sees the particular tasks of women as motherhood (1 Tim 2:15),[361] showing hospitality to strangers (1 Tim 5:10), and all sorts of acts of loving service (1 Tim 5:10). Women may give instruction, so long as it is not public teaching of the congregation, but takes place among small groups of women (Tit. 2:3–4); Paul also takes it for granted that mothers will instruct their children (*cf.* 2 Tim 3:15; 1:5).

Women's service in the congregation was of great importance for Paul. His letters prove how highly the apostle regarded women's contributions to spreading the gospel and meeting the needs of the congregation (*cf.* Rom 16:1–4, 6, 12, 13, 15; Phil 4:2–3; 1 Tim 5:5, 10). There is no passage in Paul where he disparages the service given by women. He assigns different tasks to men and women, not because he underrates women, but to preserve the different character of the sexes and their appropriate position in creation. His attitude is in complete agreement with that of Jesus, who in his teaching and actions recognised the differences between men and women. Jesus and Paul agree that creation and redemption do not conflict with each other; rather they constitute an inseparable unity, since both nature and grace are the work of God. For this reason Jesus and Paul do not abrogate the created order of the sexes in the kingdom of God, or the church, but expressly acknowledge it.

5   Man and Woman in Marriage

The divinely intended relationship between the sexes in marriage is described quite briefly in Colossians 3:18 and more fully in Ephesians 5:22–33. We shall concentrate entirely on the text from Ephesians, for it is the most sublime statement in the New Testament about marriage.

[22] Wives, be subject to your husbands, as to the Lord. [23] For the husband is the head of the wife as Christ is the head of the church, his body, and is himself its Saviour. [24] As the church is subject to Christ, so let wives also be subject in everything to their husbands. [25] Husbands, love your wives, as Christ loved the church and gave himself up for her, [26] that he might sanctify her, having cleansed her by the washing of water with the word, [27] that he might present the church to himself in splendour, without spot or wrinkle or any such thing, that she might be holy and without blemish. [28] Even so husbands should love their wives as their own bodies. He who loves his wife loves himself. [29] For no man ever hates his own flesh, but nourishes and cherishes it, as

Christ does the church, [30]because we are members of his body. [31]'For this reason a man shall leave his father and mother and be joined to his wife, and the two shall become one flesh.' [32]This mystery is a profound one, and I am saying that it refers to Christ and the church; [33]however, let each one of you love his wife as himself, and let the wife see that she respects her husband.

This text refutes all those commentators who on the basis of 1 Corinthians 7 claim that Paul disparages marriage. Could anything grander be said about matrimony than that it reflects the inner relationship between Christ and the church? At the same time the text makes it clear that the distinction between men and women cannot be reversed, as Christ and the church are and remain quite distinct from each other.

Our passage is characterised by the interweaving of 'is' and 'ought', of gift and obligation. It does not say 'the husband *should be* the head of the wife', but 'the husband *is* the head of the wife as Christ *is* the head of the church' (*cf.* 1 Cor 11:3). The husband is therefore placed over his wife constitutionally; 'being' head over his wife is just as inseparable from his nature as Christ's headship over the church.[362] Just as one cannot confess Jesus Christ without affirming his lordship, so it is impossible to confess maleness without affirming male headship. When men refuse to accept their particular responsibility to be head of the wife, they are rebelling against the position intended by God and living in contradiction to their nature as males. God has put the husband over his wife in a similar way to that in which he put Christ over the church.

Because a husband is head, there follow clearly differentiated duties for both sexes; from the *gift* of being head there follow for the husband quite distinct obligations. Our text begins with consequences for the wife. 'Wives, be subject to your husbands, as to the Lord . . . As the church is subject to Christ, so let wives also be subject in everything to their husbands' (vv. 22, 24). Also, when it comes to the consequences which follow from the husband's position as head, Paul has Christ and the church as the models in his mind's eye: as the church is totally subject to Christ, so wives are to be subject to their husbands 'in everything'. Without the comparison with Christ, the primacy of the husband 'in everything' could be misunderstood as a licence for every form of male tyranny. The comparison with Christ shows the content, character, and limits of this subjection. Christ's headship is a reign of sacrificial love. So Paul demands: 'Husbands, love your wives, as Christ loved the church and gave himself up for her, that he might sanctify her . . . Even so husbands should love their wives as their own bodies' (v. 25–6, 28). In these verses the headship of the husband is marked off as sharply as possible from any male egoism or any subjugation of the wife. Jesus' self-offering on the cross, and his life of perfect love, which included a willingness to serve as a slave (John 13:1–17), set a standard for male headship which cannot be surpassed.

It must therefore be regarded as a calamity that precisely Ephesians 5:22ff. is appealed to time and again to justify the pious assertiveness of Christian husbands; the subjection of wives is emphasised one-sidedly (vv. 22–4), but the demand for sacrificial love by the husband (vv. 25–33) is passed over. The chief emphasis of our text is not the subjection of the wife, but quite clearly the selfless love of the husband. Whereas four verses are devoted to wives (vv. 22–4, 33), nine are directed at husbands (vv. 25–33). Husbands are just as often commanded to love (vv. 25, 28, 33) as wives are told to submit (vv. 22, 24 and implicitly v. 33). Since the command to love disallows any egoism by the men, there is no text less fitted to justify arbitrary male domination than Ephesians 5:22ff.! If a husband is really head after the model of Jesus, then all oppression of wives must cease. Just as Christ as head of the church does not oppress, but is concerned for her best interests ('that she might be holy and without blemish', v. 27), so a husband's headship means he seeks the best for his wife with all his powers. It is a reign of love directed towards the well-being of the wife and the whole family.

The phrase 'in everything' (v. 24) indicates that the husband's headship relates to all areas of life. The man is called to be head in both the natural and the spiritual realms, that is to be the spiritual leader in marriage and to assume special responsibility for the ordinary affairs of life. Being head always means exercising chief responsibility in all aspects of married and family lifestyle. The husband whose headship is modelled on Christ's relieves his wife of a burden. Just as the church can take comfort from entrusting its leadership to Christ, so can a wife by letting her husband have the final say in all issues relating to the marriage. The husband, on the other hand, is obliged to relieve his wife of the burden of the final decision and responsibility before God.

Of course that does not entail the wife abjectly and passively submitting to her husband's will. Paul took it for granted that the wife's duty to obey ended where her husband was leading her into sin. Submission to the husband assumes submission to God. The injunction to submit to the husband (v. 22) presupposes wives are subject to the Lord ('as to the Lord'), and should conflict arise, without doubt obedience towards God is the decisive consideration.

The wife is not thereby absolved from the duty of thinking critically; she owes this to her husband as his God-appointed helpmeet. She has to watch and help him carry through his headship in a Christlike way. This is expressed in our text when it emphasises the unity between man and wife (vv. 28–32). Accordingly our passage speaks not just of Christ's primacy over the church, and of the husband over the wife, but also of the inner fellowship between Christ and the church, and between husband and wife. As the church is portrayed as the body of Christ (vv. 23, 29–30), so the wife is symbolically compared to her husband's body (vv. 28–9, 31). Paul interprets the 'becoming one flesh' of Genesis 2:24 symbolically, so that the husband is the head and the wife the body of this 'one flesh', just as Christ is the head and the church is his body. Paul thus views marriage as an organism which reflects the inner organic fellowship between Christ and the church. It obligates both partners to endeavour to become one in thought, will, and action. And it excludes any passive or unthinking submission by a wife to her husband's will.

This licence to criticise, which a wife owes her husband as his companion, does not of course free her from the duty to submit 'in everything' (v. 24). Our text gives no more scope for egoistical self-assertion by the wife than it does for egoistical arbitrariness by the husband. The wife is not placed alongside her husband as a second head in order to be always correcting his decisions, but is a partner subordinate to him, to whom he owes his entire love. The wife's role as helpmeet, mentioned in Genesis 2:18, is seen in the light of Ephesians 5:22ff. to be that of helping her husband to be head in the way Christ is. A wife who does not recognise that her husband is head rejects her task of being his helpmeet and rebels against the divinely intended position of the sexes.

The wife's duty to submit to her husband cannot be relativised by an appeal to verse 21, just before our passage, where church members (not marriage partners!) are exhorted to 'be subject to one another'. For the Greek phraseology does not necessarily mean a strictly mutual submission, but can also describe the appropriate respect for order that should characterise behaviour.[363] That the latter is meant is shown unmistakably by the injunctions which follow verse 21 in 5:22–6:9, in which there is 'no example of mutual submission',[364] only of unidirectional submission (Christ – Church, Husband – Wife, Parents – Children, Master – Slave). Ephesians 5:21 could therefore be paraphrased: 'Be subject to each other within the appropriate framework – wives to husbands, children to parents, slaves to masters, not indiscriminately all submitting to each other, but one submitting to the other, that is the lower to the higher.'[365]

But how is unidirectional submission of the wife to the husband to be understood? We have several times insisted that we are not dealing with an uncritical slavish submission. It is rather a conscious and free submission which arises from 'insight into a saving structure'.[366] The Greek word *hypotassesthai*, 'be subject', covers 'a complete range of meanings from submitting to an authority to a fully conscious putting oneself at the disposal of another'.[367] According to Paul the demand that a wife should be subject is based on the fact that the divinely intended relationship between men and women can be realised on in this way. This relationship corresponds to the nature of both the sexes and also serves the welfare of both. Opposition to the man being head destroys, says Paul, the basis of maleness and femaleness, as being head is inseparable from the man's being and nature (cf. 1 Cor 11:3; Eph 5:23). How little submission has to do with lack of honour is apparent in 1 Corinthians 11:3, where the submission of the woman is compared to Christ's submission to the Father. The submission expected of the woman in Ephesians 5:22 is a submission in love to the loving leadership of the husband, whose headship means he lovingly takes on all responsibility. The marriage relationship of Ephesians 5:22ff. is therefore of mutual love, which obliges the man to lead in love and the wife to follow in love.[368] It rests on the insight that the harmony God intends in marriage can be realised 'only where one takes the lead, and the other is prepared to follow. Without submission there can never be harmony.'[369]

Paul wanted to make clear in Ephesians 5:22ff. how following Christ is realised in marriage. When a Christian husband maintains headship, he is, according to Paul, following Christ in the strictest sense of the word, for when he makes real his headship by selfless love of his wife, he reflects the behaviour of Jesus Christ towards his church. For a husband, following Christ and being head cannot be separated: if one is infringed, so is the other. The Christian wife, on the other hand, is called to reflect in a special way the receptive submissive outlook of the church. According to 1 Corinthians 11:3 she then reflects the attitude of Christ to the Father. So for women too, following Christ and accepting the order set out in Ephesians 5:22ff. are inseparably linked. A wife who opposes her husband being head denies her femaleness and rebels against Christ. Ephesians 5 does not contain temporally conditioned patriarchal concepts in Christian dress, as many modern expositors maintain, but eternal truths which affect the fundamentals of Christian existence and cannot be set aside without damaging the foundations of the church (*cf.* Chapter 10).

When we compare Paul's views on marriage with his remarks about the place of the sexes within the church, we see that both are based on the same principle: the man is head of the woman and is therefore called in church life and in marriage to the task of leadership. For Paul headship in marriage and in church life are inseparable. Experience as head in marriage is according to him an indispensable prerequisite for every church leader. In 1 Timothy 3:4 he makes it a condition of leadership in the church that the candidate 'must manage his own household well'. This criterion is illuminating. For whoever is not in the position to lead a marriage or run a family will not be able to lead a church according to God's purpose.

Ephesians 5:22ff. shows that the headship of the husband is not just to be understood as a creation ordinance (as in Gen 1–3), but also as an *ordinance for the life of the redeemed church*, whose inner criterion of absolute love has been realised in the self-sacrifice of Christ on the cross. Finally, 1 Corinthians 11:3 anchors the headship of the man right in the trinitarian being of God, where there is both super- and subordination among the divine persons.

It is worth noting that in all the texts discussed Paul attempts to demonstrate his position with weighty theological arguments and not pragmatically. For Paul, opposition to the relationship between the sexes which he defends is tantamount to opposing God's creation and indeed indirectly to opposing God's trinitarian nature. To be sure, his appeal to creation shows that man's primacy over woman is conditioned by creation and is therefore valid for all, both inside and outside the church. When he models marriage on Christ's relationship to the church (Eph 5:22ff.), he makes it apparent that only Christians are really in the position to realise, however imperfectly, the divinely intended pattern of relationships between the sexes. Of course non-Christian husbands can to a degree exercise their task as head. However, in the light of Ephesians 5 it must be said that a husband who is not consecrated to Christ cannot be true to his headship. Oppression of the wife or a complete upset of the creation ordinance by a setting aside or a reversal of subordination are the unavoidable consequences if man and wife are not disciples of Christ.

8
Man and Woman in the Rest of the New Testament

The affirmation of sexuality characterises the whole New Testament. Nowhere is sex or sexuality belittled or marriage viewed as a necessary evil. The New Testament takes over the Old's affirmation of sexuality and supplements it only in one respect, namely through the sayings of Jesus (Matt 19:3–12) and Paul (1 Cor 7; 1 Tim 5:3–16) which affirm that even abstinence from sex and marriage for God's sake can be a purposeful and fulfilling way of life.

The equality of the sexes is also nowhere questioned in the New Testament. All the books of the New Testament presuppose that women are 'joint heirs of the grace of life' (1 Pet 3:7) who enjoy the same access to God, redemption in Jesus Christ, and life under the guidance of the Spirit as men do. One will search in vain in the New Testament for any disparagement or disdain of women. There is no trace in the teaching of Jesus or in the rest of the New Testament of the moral, legal and religious superiority of the male that characterised contemporary Judaism.

The differentiation of male and female is of course presupposed very decisively in the New Testament, and its practical consequences are again and again evident. The basic principles apparent in the teaching of Jesus and Paul are never questioned. It is one of the most basic convictions of the New Testament that the man is head of the woman. In the apostolic era this conviction was acknowledged as the valid basis of both church and married life, when pressures to level out the differences between the sexes had even then to be opposed publicly (*cf.* 1 Cor 11:3ff.; 14:33ff.). At any rate there is not a single passage within the New Testament that shows women having a teaching or church leadership function! It is often overlooked in this connection that 1 Corinthians 14:33ff. is not the narrow-minded individual opinion of Paul, but that it expresses the accepted practice in all the congregations of the early church (v. 34). Also the custom of head-covering in 1 Corinthians 11, often traced back to Pauline narrowness, was then a characteristic of the whole Christian community (1 Cor 11:16). It is extraordinarily important for the understanding of both passages to see that here Paul is speaking as the advocate and representative of the *whole* primitive church.

Recently some have tried to refute the thesis that there were no female apostles, teachers or church leaders in the apostolic churches with the supposition that in Romans 16:7 a female apostle named Junia is mentioned.[370]

This interpretation is however untenable, because

1. The accentuation of the word in the Greek manuscripts is with few exceptions clearly masculine.[371]

2. Given Paul's fondness for shortening names, the name is best explained as a short form, Junias, of the common man's name Junianus.[372]

3. The idea that on the one hand Paul could greet a female apostle and on the other concur with the practice of the universal church in forbidding women any kind of preaching ministry (1 Cor 14:33ff.) is historically improbable.

4. Against the hypothesis that Romans 16:7 mentions a female apostle stands the fact that not a single passage in the whole New Testament so much as hints at the existence of female apostles. Rather the gospels explicitly attest that Jesus called only men into the apostolic band. Since the person mentioned in Romans 16:7 was already a Christian before Paul, it would be necessary to make the completely improbable historical assumption that the early church very soon after the resurrection set aside their Lord's practice and admitted women to the office of apostle. This is an assumption that lacks any basis in the texts available to us. It must be

assumed that such a revolutionary innovation of the early church would surely have been mentioned by Luke, the author of Acts, who is so sympathetic to women. In Acts Luke mentions points of much lesser moment: for example, that the daughters of Philip were prophetesses (21:9), and that Priscilla with Aquila gave private instruction in the Bible to the Corinthian Jew Apollos (18:26).

These points should suffice to show the assumption that Junia was a female apostle to be completely untenable. It may also be mentioned that there is no evidence in the New Testament for women exercising teaching or leadership functions, but there are passages which allow the opposite conclusion to be drawn (*cf.* 1 Cor 14:33ff.; 1 Tim 2:12; 3:2, 5). The apostolic church obviously stuck to the pattern of Jesus and put the creation ordinance formulated in Genesis 2 into practice in the life of the congregations. This is not contradicted by the existence of prophetesses in New Testament congregations (Acts 21:9). For one thing, in the light of 1 Corinthians 14:33ff. it is doubtful whether such prophetesses brought a word to the whole church in public worship, and for another, the office of prophet is clearly distinguished from the office of apostle, teacher, or church leader. Here the New Testament stands firmly in the Old Testament tradition, for in Old Testament times the priesthood was reserved for men, although there were prominent prophetesses.

For the New Testament view of marriage 1 Peter 3:1–7 is also important. Here too the headship of the husband is presupposed. But it is novel in appreciating the wife's subordination as an evangelistic witness: 'Likewise you wives, be submissive to your husbands, so that some, though they do not obey the word, may be won without a word by the behaviour of their wives, when they see your reverent and chaste behaviour' (vv. 1–2). This statement is an earnest exhortation to those Christian wives who think that they do not have to submit to a non-Christian husband. 1 Peter 3:1–2 lets it be understood that the superior authority of the husband is a *creation ordinance* which also applies to non-Christian marriages. On the other hand, this statement offers great encouragement to believing wives to win their unbelieving husbands for Christ by their quiet and patient submission. Peter regards this mission 'without a word' as the special task of Christian wives in mixed marriages. His concern is that the wives through the inner beauty of their devotion to Christ, not through obtrusive external decoration (v. 3), should draw attention to 'the hidden person of the heart with the imperishable jewel of a gentle and quiet spirit' (v. 4). Such a life, quietly following Christ, is according to Peter 'in God's sight . . . very precious'. It contains a 'victorious power which overcomes everything and remains indestructible',[373] and is even capable of transforming husbands who are in rebellion against God.

The life of quiet peaceableness here put before women by Peter is a gift of the Holy Spirit. The woman 'becomes peaceable and quiet, because the Spirit is peaceable and quiet'.[374] Women are called to portray in a special way the placidity of Jesus (cf. Matt 11:29) and his hidden life at Nazareth. Gertrude von le Fort captures the spirit of our passage exactly when she speaks of the women's calling as 'the apostleship of silence', and of their mission 'to portray the hidden life of Christ in the church'.[375] Such a life of quiet peaceableness may totally contradict our age's noisy spirit of emancipation, but it gives women an unsuspected beauty and power to change others, because it realises their femininity in God's intended way and God's goodwill and blessing rests on them.

1 Peter 3:1–6 unfolds the picture of the divine vocation of women which is normative throughout the New Testament and is embodied with exemplary purity in Mary, the mother of our Lord. The greatness of Mary rests in her quiet willingness to let the miracle of the incarnation happen to her (cf. Luke 1:38) and to retire completely behind the mission of her son and the apostles. She was true to her divine calling, not through public activity for God but by letting God work secretly in her and by helping prepare for the public activity of her son by being a mother. The same is true for the women who were followers of Jesus. They do not step into the limelight but rather work steadily in the background (cf. Luke 8:2–3) in order to make possible the public ministry of Jesus and the apostles.

Paul's remarks about the tasks of women in the church also value highly the quiet existence for God (*cf* 1 Cor 14:35; 1 Tim 2:11; 5:13) and reject any public teaching or leadership role (1 Cor 14:33ff.; 1 Tim 2:12ff.). Behind all these comments lies the key concept of the woman as the man's helpmeet, who accompanies his public activity with quiet peaceableness and precisely through her hidden existence on God's behalf exercises a blessing which is not to be undervalued.

1 Peter 3 is free from any devaluation of women. Peter recognises the equality of women as 'joint heirs of the grace of life' (v. 7). His explanations are intended to unfold the beauty and dignity which God intended for women. For this reason he urges husbands (v. 7) to give their wives the honour which is their due. 'That is a powerful thrust against the contempt for women widespread in the Orient.'[376] Husbands are duty-bound to treat their wives with respect and considerate love. Peter urges husbands to take into account in their behaviour the lesser strength of their wives and to strive for marital fellowship 'considerately' (*i.e.*, with moderation and love). Peter states that the test of proper conduct in marriage is that the prayer life of both partners is not harmed: 'in order that your prayers may not be hindered' (v. 7). This principle is born out of deep pastoral wisdom. 'The rule, live your marriage so that you can pray, indicates very surely what is pure and important in marriage and what must be avoided.'[377] 1 Peter 3:7 shows that the spiritual fellowship of the spouses is the heart of every Christian marriage. By making the shared life of the spouses with God the basis and norm of Christian marriage, Peter creates the best foundation for husbands and wives to live as God determined, and thereby to overcome the age-long battle of the sexes by mutual self-sacrifice.

This concludes our examination of what Scripture says about men and women. Despite the great variety of biblical texts examined, an astonishing consistency has emerged. Everywhere the relationship of the sexes established at creation (Gen 1–3) is the basis. This is reinterpreted and deepened by passages in the New Testament in the light of Christ's revelation.

9
The Biblical View of Man and Woman in Church History

It would make our study far too long if we were to explore in detail the historical effects of the biblical view of the sexes on theology and church practice. Here we must therefore limit ourselves to a few comments.

1. The biblical affirmation of sexuality unfortunately did not remain uncontested in church history.[378] Already in the early church there were antisomatic tendencies abroad. From the third century the Christian sex ethic is characterised by a radical devaluation of sex, which eventually led Augustine to the view that sexual intercourse was intrinsically sinful.[379]

Pope Gregory I (c. 540–604) distinguished between sexual intercourse as such, which within marriage is not sinful, and the pleasure inevitably accompanying it, which always involves guilt.[380] This proscription of pleasure has fatefully affected the history of Christianity until recent times. Even Luther was of the opinion 'that no marital intercourse occurs without sin',[381] but that God in his mercy does not regard it as sin.[382] Zinzendorf held that the duty of spouses was to have intercourse without lust, and entirely to God's glory.[383]

It would take us too long to reproduce the lengthy list of remarks by Christian theologians against sex. It is certainly one of the shameful chapters of church history in which Christendom under the influence of pagan and Greek ideas has often distanced itself from the biblical affirmation of sexuality. Nevertheless care must be taken not to overstate the extent of this unfortunate Christian opposition to sex, because the biblical affirmation of the sexual has left many examples of its influence on Christendom.[384] Christian art includes many works which express an outspoken uninhibited attitude to the human body. The earliest Christian art (paintings from the catacombs, sculpture on sarcophagi) is not afraid to portray naked human bodies. In the first Christian centuries the church showed itself quite unembarrassed at the administration of baptism: candidates of all ages were baptised unclothed! It seems that in the early days of the Church they succeeded in combining naturalness and modesty. In later times we still find indications of Christians viewing their bodies without embarrassment. For example, at the beginning of the twentieth century 'Italian mothers pacified their children at the breast quite unembarrassed even in church' and 'coloured Christians went to worship almost naked'.[385] These indications, which could be multiplied, suffice to show that the antisomatic tendencies of Christendom were not enough to suppress completely the biblical affirmation of sexuality. It is sad, though, that such tendencies were able to gain so much influence and injured the health of many Christians. The sex tide now swamping the so-called Christian West is a reaction to the pseudo-Christian antipathy to the body, a reaction which nonetheless, through its divinisation of lust, is even more disastrously removed from biblical standards.

2. The equality of the sexes attested in the Bible has also not always been maintained in Christendom. Church history contains grave witnesses to the devaluation of women.[386] Time and again the woman has been put down as morally inferior to the man, as 'the devil's point of entry' (Tertullian) which men ought to beware of.[387] The most horrific form of misogyny was the centuries-long persecution of witches, in which perhaps more than a million women died.[388]

But at least Christian theologians upheld, with rare exceptions, that the woman is the equal of the man. The high value that Jesus gave to women had an enduring influence on the history of the Christian church and theology. Christianity did away with the religious undervaluation of women once and for all. That women, like men, enjoyed through faith access to eternal salvation was never questioned in Christendom. For the conviction of sexual equality is so central to the gospel that its denial would involve a denial of the saving message.

While the church maintained that indissoluble monogamy as taught by Christ was the only legitimate form of sexual cohabitation, it emphatically stood up for the dignity of women and effectively protected them against the advantages which married men enjoyed under ancient marriage law. Through Jesus' love-command, the heart of Christian ethics, the church was protected from viewing marriage simply as a legal institution for producing children. It was viewed rather as a fellowship of unconditional love and fidelity, in which man *and* wife could experience happiness, security and fulfilment in highest measure.

Even if Christian reality did not always correspond to Christian convictions, women experienced within the church a quite remarkable respect and dignity. This becomes even clearer when it is compared with the situation of women in antiquity before Christ came.[389] One sign of the value of women in Christendom is that in the early church, at least from the second century, more women confessed the Christian faith than did men.[390] This preponderance of women led to the early church being despised as 'the religion of the poor and the women' (*religio pauperum et mulierum*).[391] Within the churches women found an opportunity to live as highly valued persons and to be taken seriously as 'sisters in Christ' who belong to God's redeemed family. How highly they were valued is shown by the fact that women martyrs, of whom there were a great many, were held in just as high honour as men who died for the faith. The records of the martyrs are a striking witness to the regard in which the women of Christendom were held. The church offered women an unrestricted share not only in Christ's salvation, in worship and in the sacraments, but also in important spheres of service for God (see below). In this respect the character of women as men's equals as depicted in the New Testament is fully acknowledged.

3. The differences between the sexes that are explicit in the

Bible, and their consequent differentiation of tasks within the church, remained uncontested in Christendom (with only a few trivial exceptions) until the twentieth century. This is most obvious in the way that Catholic, Orthodox and Protestant Christendom followed the New Testament by limiting teaching and leadership functions in the church to men. In the early church this practice was disregarded only by heretical movements such as Montanism,[392] Quintillianism[393] and Gnosticism.[394] The exclusion of women from the office of preaching and teaching by no means condemned them to inactivity. The early church, following the New Testament (*cf.* Rom 16:1–2; 1 Tim 5:3–16), created for unmarried women the office of *deaconess*, which comprised a variety of activities such as caring for the sick, social and pastoral care of women, assisting at the baptism of women and preparing them for it.[395] With the office of deaconess Christianity opened up a sphere of activity for Christian women which was closed to women both in Judaism and in other religions.[396] Indeed the office of deaconess was allowed to continue in the Western church until the fourth century, while it continued in the East until the twelfth century.[397] This later exclusion of women from church office was mitigated when the Middle Ages opened up a new large sphere of activity for women, for example in education. The caring work of the deaconesses of the early church was revived in the orders of Catholic women (from the sixteenth century) and in the Protestant order of deaconesses (from the nineteenth century).

We see, then, that Christendom largely retained the distribution of church offices between the sexes according to the guidelines established by the New Testament. This is also true of the prophetesses permitted in the New Testament.[398] Whereas there were hardly any prophets in the Catholic church after the second century, the church again and again permitted charismatically endowed women to act as prophetesses. Women such as Hildegard of Bingen (1098–1179), the 'Teutonic prophetess', and Catherine of Siena (1347–80) were allowed to act in this way without thereby being allowed to participate directly in the office of pastor. It was left to our century to break much more extensively with nearly two thousand years of tradition going back to the New Testament by permitting women to take charge of a congregation,[399] and more recently to open even the episcopal office to women,[400] thereby putting in question the distinction of male and female offices within the church. This development of course occurred first in the Protestant churches, whereas the Catholic and Orthodox churches have until now decisively opposed it. This raises the basic question whether and how far the New Testament view of the sexes is still valid and binding for church life.

10
The Continuing Validity of the Biblical View of Man and Woman

In our age more and more theologians are arguing that the biblical view of man and woman is determined by its patriarchal environment and is therefore in need of revision. In particular the subordination of women to men and their exclusion from church teaching and leadership offices have attracted criticism and rejection. We now want to demonstrate more thoroughly why the biblical ordering of the sexes is still valid and why its surrender threatens central truths of the Christian faith.

In the face of the superficiality and ease with which some reject the statements of Holy Scripture, it is necessary to point out that the burden of proof lies on those who reject the contents of the Bible, not on those who uphold the traditional standpoint. This is true both of those who question the biblical record of history as well as those who question the Bible's teaching. The Bible is among Christians the accepted authority in all questions of life and doctrine. So it is not the affirmation but the rejection of biblical statements that requires to be justified. Today this is often overlooked or paid insufficient attention. Nevertheless it is the continuing important task of Christian theology not just to assert the abiding validity of biblical teaching, but also to demonstrate it. This should lead to a deeper understanding of biblical theology and prevent it from being misunderstood. This is the purpose of the following discussions. They are intended to help all those who are concerned to achieve a deeper understanding of Holy Scripture.

There are four reasons for maintaining the biblical ordering of male and female.

1   Its Claim to be Based on Revelation

The biblical view of the sexes claims to be based on revelation. To maintain that the biblical ordering of the sexes, as found in Genesis 1–3 and developed in the New Testament, is culturally conditioned contradicts the Bible's own claim.

There is no doubt that in both testaments a text like Genesis 1–3 is viewed as a revelation about men and women that continues to be valid. The way in which both Jesus (Matt 19:4–5) and Paul (Eph 5:31; 1 Tim 2:13–14) direct attention to the first three chapters of the Bible shows that they see them as texts revealing divine norms, which disclose valid truth about mankind and his sexuality. Indeed Jesus on the basis of Genesis 1 and 2 goes so far as to reject the husband's right of divorce which the Old Testament explicitly allows (Deut 24:1–4), because it contradicts the original intention of God the creator. This passage shows that Jesus regards Genesis 1 and 2 as expressing God's creation ordinance, which remains valid. Indeed it implies that the Old Testament may be criticised by the standards expressed in Genesis 1–2.

The New Testament texts about the ordering of male and female also include within them the claim that they are not culturally conditioned attitudes which need to be revised; they are rather truths of revelation that are still valid. This is particularly obvious in the theological reasons that are cited in Pauline texts such as 1 Corinthians 11:3ff.; 14:33ff. or Ephesians 5:22ff. Paul anchors his view of male and female in the nature of God (1 Cor 11:3), in Christ's work of redemption (Eph 5:22ff.), in the nature of the sexes (1 Cor 11:3ff.; Eph 5:22ff.). He appeals to the divine creation ordinance (1 Cor 11:8–9; 1 Tim 2:13–14) and to a command of the Lord (1 Cor 14:37). All this makes it clear that Paul professes to be passing on abiding truths whose rejection involves opposing

God (cf. 1 Cor 14:37). Paul is of course aware of the difference between the truths of revelation which he stands for and the customs to which they give rise (1 Cor 11:16). The theological ordering of man and woman is not on the same level as the culturally conditioned church customs which are derived from them. It is necessary, though, that church order and custom do not contradict God's intended ordering of the sexes, but rather express it. That is the reason why Paul fights so strongly for the custom of covering the head, because he regards setting it aside as rebellion against a creation ordinance that remains valid.

In all the Pauline texts we are faced with the fact that for the apostle the headship of the man represents an unassailable natural ordinance that is based on God's creative will. To reject this ordinance is to rebel against God, and this cannot be tolerated in the church. Male headship as advocated by Paul does not chime in just with Genesis 1–3, but is also in agreement with Christ (cf. above pp. 98–101) and all the rest of the New Testament (cf. above pp. 130–4). It is precisely those controversial passages such as 1 Corinthians 11:3ff. and 1 Corinthians 14:33ff. about the organisation of the church reflecting male headship which show that Paul fully agrees with the whole church of his time (1 Cor 11:16; 14:33).

All this leads to the following important conclusion. To hold that the biblical ordering of the sexes is culturally conditioned and therefore changeable is to contradict Scripture's own claim. The relevant biblical texts do not argue pragmatically from the contemporary social situation; on the contrary, they claim to be passing on binding revealed truth. An interpretation which does not take seriously this claim that the biblical texts make loses credibility and cannot be taken seriously in theology.

The early church took seriously the claim about the biblical ordering of male and female not just in church life, by giving the pastoral and teaching offices to men, but also in their theology. This is seen, for example, in the way that well-known fathers of the early church very early accepted the New Testament ethical lists as canonical, that is as a normative Word of God.[401] Male headship was not only undisputed in the theology of the early church and the Middle Ages, but was also defended in the modern period by the overwhelming majority of significant systematic theologians until the mid-twentieth century. Adolf Schlatter,[402] Karl Barth,[403] Emil Brunner[404] and Dietrich Bonhoeffer,[405] to name just a few of the most important Protestant theologians of the twentieth century, saw in the biblical ordering of the sexes an abidingly valid truth. So whoever regards the New Testament ordering of male and female as outdated is not just breaking with the New Testament at this point, but with the tradition of the church of nearly two thousand years.

2   The Impossibility of Deriving it from the Contemporary World

The biblical view of man and woman was not derived from the surrounding contemporary culture. It is asserted again and again that the biblical view of man and woman is derived from the patriarchal ideas of that era. However, this assertion founders on the fact that the biblical view is distinctively different from the convictions of the surrounding culture. We shall try to demonstrate this by a few examples.

If, for example, Genesis 2 is compared with similar extra-biblical texts of the same period, it appears that this chapter is 'unique' in the high value it assigns to woman 'among the creation myths of the whole of the Ancient Near East'.[406] Furthermore, Genesis 1–3 expresses the equality of the sexes with such conviction (cf. above pp. 63–8) that even the rest of the Old Testament and the life of ancient Israel did not maintain it entirely. Genesis 1–3 is thus not just unique in the ancient Near East, it is also special within the Old Testament.

The exclusion of women from the Old Testament priesthood seems to be a convincing example of the patriarchal ideas of the ancient world influencing the biblical ordering of male and female. But this example proves the very opposite.

With the rejection of a female priesthood Israel sharply conflicted with the practice of the ancient Orient, where priestesses were taken for granted.[407] This cannot be explained as just intended to avoid the contemporary practice of cult prostitution, for sacred prostitution was by no means confined to women in the ancient Near East.[408] As will be explained,[409] this rejection is of a piece with the Old Testament doctrine of God.[410] Similarly, the New Testament's exclusion of women from church teaching and leadership is plainly continuous with the Old Testament limitation of the priesthood to men.

It is true that the apostles, teachers, and church leaders in Christianity did not fulfil the narrowly priestly functions, such as offering sacrifice, but they were like the Old Testament priests in being spiritual leaders and teachers. In the light of the tendencies towards female emancipation[411] and the high value put on female priests[412] by other religions in the apostolic era this represents a striking break with the contemporary world:

> [when] incipient Christianity, despite its rejection of so many Jewish customs and its broadminded openness to the Gentile world, maintained the biblical and Jewish tradition . . . When the Hebrew, Jewish and finally Christian priesthood is put in its historical context, it becomes evident that the persistent rejection of a female priesthood has nothing to do with contemporary practices or prejudice. It derives rather from a lasting, quite conscious contradiction of what the whole world perceived as normal.[413]

In the light of the historical evidence we are in fact not justified in deriving the Old Testament limitation of the priesthood to men from the contemporary world. The same is true of the New Testament restriction of pastoral and teaching offices to men. One could, though, try to derive New Testament practice not from the Greco-Roman world, but from the Jewish environment. But this fails because the New Testament's exclusion of women from teaching and leadership positions goes back to the practice of Jesus, who only called men as apostles. His approach was totally free of any opportunistic or pragmatic accommodation with the Judaism of his day. However one looks at it, the fact remains: the exclusion of women from the pastoral and preaching ministry in the New Testament does not depend on the world in which Christianity first developed, but it rests on a practice based on important theological reasons (the example of Jesus, the Old Testament priesthood, and creation ordinances).

The fashionable attempt to trace the tradition behind the New Testament's ethical lists (*e.g.*, Eph 5:22ff.) back to the lists of duties current in Hellenistic Judaism and moral philosophy also does not stand up to closer investigation. There are certainly *formal* parallels, in that in both cases the duties of household members are portrayed. 'A thorough and comprehensive study of the available material shows, however, that the New Testament's ethical lists, despite all their formal affinity with their parallels in Hellenistic paranesis, are really quite distinctive.'[414] Even in their formal aspect there are striking differences. The Hellenistic catalogues of duties are wordier and lengthier, and as a rule deal not just with members of the household, but with individual classes and their duties towards the gods, relatives, and friends. The New Testament lists, on the other hand, are characterised by pregnant brevity and concentration on the essentials.[415] However, the decisive difference is found in the content of these lists. The exhortations to household members (husbands, wives, children, slaves) do not merely offer a Christian motivation, they are in essence specifically Christian. This is quite obvious in Ephesians 5:22ff. Placing the husband over the wife in marriage is not simply justified on the ground that Christ's relationship with the church is a model for human marriage. Rather this justification is of decisive importance for the character and style of the husband's primacy. His primacy is characterised by a sacrificial love like Christ's. It is obvious that a text like Ephesians 5:22ff., which is so intensely rooted in Christ's self-sacrifice on the cross, is not derived from the non-Christian world. A demand for such selfless and sacrificial love on the part of the husband is found nowhere else. The New Testament scholar H. Greeven states that 'nowhere else in the New Testament world is it demanded that a husband should show *agapē* towards his wife. This is something quite new.'[416]

The injunction in the ethical lists that the wife should submit to her husband (Eph 5:22–4; Col 3:18) also has nothing to do with submission in the surrounding Hellenistic world. In the ethical lists the wife is not handed over into the arbitrary control of her husband. She is only obliged to submit to him 'in the Lord' (Col 3:18; *cf.* Eph 5:22), that is in so far as submitting fits in with God's will. This limitation on the wife's submission, taken in conjunction with the command that the husband should love his wife sacrificially, puts a great distance between it and the dictatorial position of the husband in the non-Christian world. For example, the Roman father had an absolute legal authority (*patria potestas*) over his wife and children, which theoretically included the right to kill members of the family.[417]

These remarks should suffice to make clear that the New Testament ethical lists are not derivable from the contemporary world. Our interpretation is also confirmed by the early church, which saw the ethical lists as something quite distinctive and explicitly apostolic that characteristically distinguished the church from the surrounding pagan world.[418]

All this leads to an important conclusion: the biblical view of man and woman is independent and distinct from the approaches of the surrounding world, so that it cannot be derived from them. Because the biblical ordering of the sexes is not derived from the surrounding world, this confirms the texts' own claim not to be human opinion but a divine revelation about male and female.

3   Its Basis in the Nature of the Sexes

The biblical view of the sexes rests on a perception into the nature of male and female. It is therefore fully compatible with what we know about the character of the sexes both from human experience and scientific investigation. That is not to say that the biblical ordering of the sexes can be adequately based on empirical knowledge about male and female, but that experimental knowledge about the sexes confirms and supports the biblical view. For the biblical outlook on male and female does not arise out of human observation but divine revelation. It can, though, if need be, be supported by human experience. It is, for example, impossible to derive the similarity of the husband–wife relationship with the union of Christ and the church from a scientific investigation of the sexes. But this does not mean that the biblical view of man and woman is beyond empirical verification. Indeed assured experimental knowledge about the sexes supports the biblical point of view in a remarkable way.

The Bible sees the man as the head of the woman. This corresponds to empirically determined characteristics of the male, his greater drive to lead and direct, his markedly dominating behaviour, his strength of will and his greater aggressiveness. In Genesis 1–3 the man is specially commissioned to subdue the earth, to open it up and organise it. This fits in with his stronger and more robust physique, with his greater ability for abstract thinking, with his particular capability for creative and pioneering achievements in all areas of intellectual life, and with his more pronounced interest in the world of things.[419]

On the other hand, Scripture characterises woman as man's *helper*. This also fits in with the scientific characterisation of woman: she is more ready and capable of adapting, she has a greater capacity to sympathise. Her superior imitative ability, including linguistic ability, and her stronger interest in people[420] destine her for the role of completing the man by being his companion. These characteristics also help her to fulfil the task of motherhood which the Bible and her physique assign her.

These few remarks should suffice to show the fundamental agreement between the biblical ideals of masculinity and the empirically determined character of the sexes. The scientifically established differences between the sexes are a vivid commentary on the picture drawn by the Bible of male and female.

How the biblical ordering of the sexes fully matches the nature of man and woman is shown by the experience of Christians who have put the biblical view of marriage and family into practice. To cite one example among many: a Lutheran church in the USA experienced a deep spiritual renewal, rediscovered the biblical guidelines for marriage and family life, and has since practised them with great blessing.[421] Examples could be multiplied. Wherever men and women were ready in all seriousness to model their marriage along New Testament lines, they have made the joyful discovery that the biblical ordering of the sexes enhanced life for both of them.

The biblical view of man and woman has of course been put in a bad light by being misused to justify male egoism, whenever husbands have taken seriously their primacy over their wives but not their duty of selfless love. So terrible distortions of 'Christian' marriages have resulted. But they in no way undermine the abundance of positive examples.

That the biblical ordering of male and female is right is confirmed by many observations of the consequences of its rejection. For example, psychiatric investigations[422] have shown that families in which the father does not lead, but defers to the mother, are psychologically and emotionally disturbed. Sons in such families tend to misbehave and fail to achieve as well as they should. In addition the children of such families tend to grow up inadequately equipped to cope with life's problems. These experimental results show how destructive are the effects of a husband's failing to fulfil his responsibility to be head of the family unit. He damages not just his family as a whole but particularly his marriage. The currently acclaimed democratic model of marriage, where the partners do not have clearly demarcated areas of competence, demonstrably leads to dissatisfaction. It is also constantly threatened by the danger of the marriage becoming a 'battleground' where again and again there are 'disputes about carrying out decisions'.[423]

All this tends to show what negative consequences ensue when the man's leadership as husband and father, which is set out in the Bible, is rejected. Whether men fulfil their headship as envisaged in the creation ordinance is of incalculable significance in marriages, families and in national life. The fundamental significance of the father attested in the Bible is confirmed by scientific discoveries about the development of human personality. It is certain that the father has a predominant influence on the personality development of a growing child (especially of boys), an influence that cannot be replaced by the mother.[424] A disturbed relationship with the father often leads to severe psychological disorders.[425] Clinical experience shows that 'the more a child is deprived of its father, and the earlier this deprivation occurs, the greater is the risk of mental illness'.[426] These surprising facts do not however weaken the fundamental significance and the irreplaceable nature of the maternal role, most obviously in the earliest childhood years. But they do show explicitly how the Bible corresponds with reality when it emphasises the special responsibilities of men.

The growing rejection by today's women of their God-given task of motherhood and the simultaneous increase in working mothers have consequences that are as destructive as husbands rejecting their special responsibility for leading in marriage and family. Thorough statistical surveys in many countries have shown that the increasing employment of women is closely connected to the increasing numbers of murders and suicides[427] – something that is not surprising, since inadequate maternal care of children must necessarily cause them psychological damage. Psychological and behavioural investigations have adequately shown that it is vital for the whole subsequent life of children for them to be closely looked after by their mother, especially when they are small.[428]

Biology professor Bernard Hassenstein writes in his remarkable book *Behavioural Biology of the Child* that 'contrary to previous views, the destiny of an infant at the age of two or three months is already dependent on the behaviour of the one who cares for it. Hitherto it was held that all that mattered was feeding, prevention of disease, and the baby's physical well being.' According to Hassenstein

> this new knowledge about the importance of an individual permanent carer in the first year of life necessitates a real revolution in the private and public care of infants, comparable to the profound reorganisation of health care that followed the discovery of the causes of the most dangerous infectious diseases (Tuberculosis 1888) and the discovery of vaccination (compulsory smallpox vaccination from 1807). The task of the immediate future is to root out maternal deprivation and its consequences with the same thoroughness with which in the past puerperal fever was conquered through hygiene and poliomyelitis through innoculation.[429]

The famous psychologist Christa Meves has written:

> All observations on individuals, every comparison with the higher mammals and ethnological statistics confirm the uncomfortable truth that children need the total personal attention of their mother if we want to avoid the risk of severe mental and physical disadvantages. A child is 7.5 times more likely to become a juvenile offender if he has lacked a constant maternal presence in the first year of his life than for any other reason.[430]

The mother's job in a child's first years is so demanding that the pursuit of a career cannot be combined with it without serious damage to the child. Investigations on children brought up in children's homes, where there are usually changing carers for them to relate to, have shown that they have suffered horrific damage as a result. On the other hand, a child born in prison and then looked after there by its mother, showed no signs of retardation or disturbance after eighteen months.[431]

Maternal care of infants cannot be taken over by the father.

Physiologically (feeding) and psychologically (sympathy and relating to people) the woman is incomparably better equipped for this task than the man. The French psychiatrist B. Muldworf writes that 'the female character, her inner drive, the tone of her voice as well as specific psychological characteristics, fit the woman better than the man to fulfil the maternal function towards the new-born child'.[432] The modern tendency to reject the divinely ordained arrangement of the sexes and to deny so far as possible the gender-specific tasks founders in this case on the rock of reality.

It is overwhelmingly important for children's emotional development (especially for adolescents' identification with their own sex) that their parents offer positive and convincing models of what it means to live as men and women. Without such models, where the parents consciously or unconsciously do not allow their maleness or femaleness to develop or indeed suppress it, there is the danger that the child will grow up to be a homosexual.[433] Or there is the risk that in adult life he or she will have difficulties building a responsible and faithful partnership with someone of the opposite sex.[434] Today's prevalent tendency to level out sexual differences must therefore be regarded as posing a serious danger to the rising generation, as this tendency considerably damages their emotional development and therefore their future prospects. In this connection it is worth reflecting that already 50% of school children in West Germany show signs of behavioural disturbance (20%) or abnormality (30%).[435] For this development the widespread neglect of paternal and maternal duties is no doubt largely to blame.

All these observations lead our discussion to an important conclusion. The continuing validity of the biblical view of man and woman is positively confirmed, first by its agreement with empirical knowledge about gender characteristics and second by Christian practice which proves it enhances life. It is negatively confirmed in that its rejection has proved destructive in various ways.

4 Its Basis in the Nature of God

The fundamental basis for the biblical view of man and woman is the nature of God as it is disclosed in the biblical revelation: the biblical view of man and woman is rooted in the nature of God. This fact will certainly surprise many readers, so we now intend to clarify and establish it.

Earlier (pp. 143–4) we indicated that the restriction of the Old Testament priesthood to men was connected with the Old Testament view of God. It views priests in a special way as *God's representatives* and therefore as reflecting his holiness and perfection. So their outer form (*cf.* Lev 21:17–21) and their ethical behaviour (*cf.* Lev 10:1–3; 21:7–15) must depict symbolically God's holy and perfect nature. In the New Testament the idea emerges that the apostles are *representatives of God or Jesus*: 'He who receives you receives me, and he who receives me receives him who sent me' (Matt 10:40; *cf.* Luke 10:16; John 13:20). As Jesus represents the Father (*cf.* John 14:9: 'He who has seen me has seen the Father'), so the apostles represent Jesus: 'As the Father has sent me, even so I send you' (John 20:21). As Christ's representatives the apostles must firstly pass on his message without distortion, and secondly by their ethical behaviour must be a visible image of Christ. The apostle Paul can even say: 'Be imitators of me, as I am of Christ' (1 Cor 11:1; *cf.* 1 Cor 4:16; Phil 3:17; 1 Thess 1:6). It is an indispensable prerequisite for church leadership in the New Testament that leaders are by their lives proven examples to the church (*cf.* 1 Tim 3:1–7; 1 Pet 5:2–3). All this shows that in the Old and New Testaments the leaders of the church (priests – OT; apostles, church leaders – NT) are seen as representatives of God (or Christ) in their life and teaching.

Consequently it follows from the biblical view of God that the leaders of the church must be men. For since in the Old and New Testaments God is depicted exclusively in male terms (as 'Father', 'Lord', 'King', *etc.*), it is natural that he must be represented by men and not by women. It is true that in a few passages God is compared to a mother (*cf.* Isa 66:13;

49:15; Ps 27:10), but in striking contrast to many religions he is nowhere termed mother. This cannot be accidental! For whereas in non-Christian religions many gods are called ' "Fathers and mothers" of mankind, or of all things . . . the Bible never says that God is "our Father and our Mother". No one who knows the entire flow of biblical revelation can maintain that this is a mere oversight.'[436] To pray to God as mother would have been totally inconceivable to the pious of the Old and New Testaments. This would be no longer the God of Israel or the Father of Jesus Christ! Because God, as revealed in Jesus' preaching, is really father (and not mother), Jesus must, as the real image of God, be son (and not daughter). Therefore Christ in his incarnation could only have become a man and not a woman, and therefore his apostles as representatives of their Lord must have been men. We see, then, how deeply rooted in the nature of God is the restriction of the apostolic office (cf. OT priesthood) to men. The God revealed in the Bible cannot be represented in the same way by men and by women! If God could be portrayed just as well by women as by men, then he could as well be addressed in prayer as 'mother', 'creatoress', or 'Lady'. Then Christ could just as well be described as God's daughter as God's son. Then Christ could just as well have become a woman as a man. We would then no longer be dealing with the God of Scripture, for its descriptions of God and Christ completely exclude the picture of God just outlined.

The famous Anglican author and lay theologian C. S. Lewis rightly pointed out that

> if all these supposals were ever carried into effect [describing God as mother and Jesus as daughter], we should be embarked on a different religion . . . a child who had been taught to pray to a Mother in Heaven would have a religious life radically different from that of a Christian child.[437]

It is a most revolutionary development in Christian theological history that in our day some Christian theologians are demanding a total revision of the biblical view of God in the way described above. Jelsma maintains that 'God is both male and female',[438] Röper that God is 'simultaneously male and female, father and mother'.[439] And if terms like 'Jesus Christ' (masculine in Greek) or 'Messiah' were replaced by the expression 'Messiah-couple' (so Marti) and 'Jesa Christa' (feminine in Greek) (so Eggimann),[440] they would lose their evident onesidedness.

But it is not difficult to see that such ideas not only break with the biblical view of God but with two thousand years of Christian theology. Here the picture of God based on God's self-revelation of himself is being replaced by a view of God nourished by the intellectual streams of feminism. Feminist theologians try to justify themselves by maintaining that the biblical view of God rests only partially on divine revelation, that the biblical authors have transferred their patriarchal attitudes to God and thereby produced a one-sided patriarchal picture of God.[441] This must of course also be true of Jesus, for he too describes God exclusively in male categories. So next we want to demonstrate more carefully why Jesus' and Scripture's male view of God is appropriate to the divine nature and indeed reflects it, and therefore cannot be ascribed to culturally determined views of patriarchy.

The central problem may be put this way. Are the masculine terms used for God in the Bible just optional descriptions, which could without loss of meaning be replaced, or at least completed by, feminine terminology? Or are they necessary descriptions, without which God's nature could not be appropriately expressed? Could one, for example, instead of praying 'Our Father' as well pray 'Our Mother'? Or would this be totally unsuitable in a prayer to the living God? If God is really both male and female, father and mother, then one could just as well pray 'Our Mother' as 'Our Father'.

We want to examine two masculine terms, 'father' and 'bridegroom', which are used to describe God in Scripture, to see whether they can be replaced or supplemented by the corresponding feminine terms 'mother' and 'bride'. We have chosen these terms because they are in themselves gender-specific, in contrast to such terms for God as 'King', 'Lord' or 'Creator'.

a God as Father

The Old Testament already calls God Father. There the term is not to be understood in the sense of a direct fatherhood by procreation, but it is identical with the concept of a creator (*cf.* Deut 32:6, 18; Isa 43:6–7; 45:5ff; 64:8; Mal 2:10) or adoptive father (Ps 2:7; 2 Sam 7:14). It is through God's revelation in Christ that we first learn that God is in his essential nature a father (*i.e.*, through begetting his Son, Jesus Christ). According to the Catholic theologian Heinrich David:

> Christ's new revelation about God consists in his being in a real sense, through begetting, a father. God may not just be pictured as father as in the Old Testament and in pagan philosophy, but on the contrary he is father in the most original sense of the word, so that 'from him all fatherhood in heaven and on earth is named'. He is the model of fatherhood and not merely termed father derivatively. For this is the content of Christ's new revelation about God, that in Christ he has a Son, that he begets, not creates, eternally.[442]

These statements of David aptly show that Jesus does not just compare God to father but that he terms him father because he is essentially father and cannot be termed anything else. Jesus' address to the Father ('Abba') is therefore not an optional one which may be replaced by any other (*e.g.*, creator or mother), but for Christ it is the only appropriate designation for God. Why could Jesus not have called God 'mother' as well? This question answers itself if one considers the nature of fatherhood and motherhood. Fatherhood involves the active procreation of new life, whereas motherhood is characterised by the overwhelmingly passive acts of conceiving, carrying, and bearing new life. Whoever ascribes motherhood to God introduces ideas into the concept of God that are completely foreign to his nature.

God's begetting (unlike human begetting) requires no maternal conception, pregnancy or giving birth. His begetting is sufficient in itself. So the description of God as mother is absolutely inappropriate.

Even the human idea of fatherhood only suits God's fatherhood imperfectly. Whereas human fatherhood is only realised through a woman's motherhood, God's fatherhood is totally independent of mediation through any other being. Therefore the New Testament does not derive divine fatherhood from human fatherhood, but rather the reverse! Human fatherhood reflects God's original and perfect fatherhood. As Ephesians 3:15 puts it, from God 'all fatherhood in heaven and on earth derives its name' (NIV mg.).

These considerations show that the living God revealed by Jesus Christ cannot be termed mother, since this term does not properly characterise his nature. We can therefore understand why Scripture never terms God mother or addresses God in this way. This fact is a necessary ingredient of the biblical revelation about God and is not to be explained by the alleged patriarchalism of Holy Scripture. Therefore when feminist theology pleads for God to be addressed as mother, it is no longer originating from the living God, but from an artificial humanly constructed idea of God. A theology flowing from feminist ideas of God can therefore no longer be seriously regarded as Christian.

But this does not mean that the ray of truth in the modern plea to call God mother can be ignored. Even if God cannot be called mother, his behaviour towards mankind may be compared with the loving behaviour of a mother, as Scripture does sometimes, though not often (cf. Isa 66:13: 'As one whom his mother comforts, so I will comfort you'). In so far as a mother brings up her children with devotion and love, she is a beautiful reflection of God's patient love. In this respect God's nature displays some psychological attributes of motherhood. But these maternal features in God are parts of his paternal love and cannot be separated from it. God's fatherliness includes in their original perfection everything possible in the way of motherly tenderness, security and love.

We therefore do not need to complete the concept of God as father by adding that of mother. Rather, all that is required is a sufficiently comprehensive concept of God's fatherhood that is capable of including the complete fullness, depth and tenderness of the perfect divine love.

b God as Bridegroom (Husband)

In the Old Testament God is often portrayed as Israel's bridegroom (Jer 2:2) or husband (*cf* Isa 54:5ff.; Jer 3:8-9; 9:2; Ezek 16; Hos 1-3). It is true that he is hardly ever directly termed Israel's husband (*cf*. Isa 54:5), but the idea is a most important feature of Old Testament prophecy. The covenant between Yahweh and his people is not just compared to a marriage, but it is described directly as a marriage covenant (*cf*. Isa 54:4ff.; Jer 3:8).

In the New Testament Jesus is frequently characterised as the bridegroom (Matt 9:15-16 and parallels; 22: 2-4 and parallels; 25:1-10; John 3:29; Rev 19:7, 9; 21:2, 9; 22:17) or as the husband of his church (Eph 5:22ff.). Again here the relationship between Christ and the church is not compared to an earthly marriage, but is viewed as a real marriage covenant. In Ephesians 5:22ff. the fellowship between Christ and the church is seen as the model for earthly marriage.

As with the concept of father, we want to ask here whether the masculine term 'husband' for God can be replaced or at least supplemented by the feminine term 'wife'. To put it another way: Could one speak fittingly of the church as bridegroom and term God the Father or Jesus Christ, who lived on earth as man, bride? It is very easy to see how absurd such a swap of terms would be. To call God husband is to describe him as the one who made the church his beloved partner in an unbreakable fellowship, and to call the church his wife is to characterise her as the recipient and target of divine love and faithfulness. To swap the terms would make God dependent on the love of the church and to put the church in the place of God. Since the covenant between God and the church is founded entirely on God's sovereign will, who chose, redeemed, and made the church his beloved spouse, only the male term 'husband' is suited to describe such a God. So, in this case too, the attempt to express God's nature through feminine terminology comes to grief.

Our study of the biblical description of God as father and bridegroom has shown that the masculine terminology of the Bible is based on the nature of God, whereas feminine terms are unsuited to designating the divine nature. For if because of his nature God may be termed father or bridegroom, but not mother or bride, then the possibility of using any other feminine terms for God, such as lady, or queen, also lapses. The masculine-shaped picture of God in Scripture is therefore not a result of its patriarchal thinking, but the result of the self-revelation of the living God! Feminist theology makes the questionable attempt to correct arbitrarily God's self-revelation in line with the spirit of the age. Such a theology affects the foundation of the Christian faith and has forfeited its right to exist within the Christian church.

The masculine-shaped picture of God in Scripture has a necessary consequence that man in his maleness is in a special way the reflection and representative of God, whereas the woman in a special way reflects and represents the creation and the redeemed church. In Genesis 2 the man is portrayed as the 'source and goal of the woman just as God is the source and goal of the whole creation',[443] for Eve was taken from the man and created for him. The relationship of man to woman is therefore according to Genesis 2 comparable to that between creator and creation. Heinrich David formulates it aptly: 'The nature of the person as male consists in him being the reflection of God as the source and goal of everything.'[444] This special representation of God through the man is specially apparent in the male as father. As father the man reflects God's essential fatherhood, even if imperfectly, since in order to be a father he needs the woman. The man also reflects God as bridegroom, in so far as he reflects God's electing love, which contracts an unbreakable bond with his partner (Israel, the church). The man's special depiction of

God does not depend on him actually becoming a father or a bridegroom in a physical sense, for in being a father or bridegroom the man's essential nature comes to bodily expression, and this essential nature characterises unmarried men as well and can also take shape in the life of the single.[445]

As the bride of Christ the woman reflects in a special way the creation and the church. As the creation is subordinate to the creator and was created for him (cf. Col 1:16), so the woman is subordinate to the man and designed for him (cf. Gen 2). The medieval mystic Hildegard of Bingen (1098–1179) put it beautifully: 'The creation looks at her creator as the loved one looks at her lover.'[446] Women are therefore called to portray the creation as loved by the creator. The receptive nature of the female makes her a unique reflection of creation, which lives entirely by receiving the divine love, and equally a reflection of the church (cf. Eph 5:22ff.), whose existence depends entirely on receiving the electing, redeeming and sanctifying love of God. It is precisely as wife that the woman is capable of portraying in unsurpassable fashion the church. Just as the church has entered into a covenant of unbreakable loyalty, so too the woman is received by her husband into an indissoluble bond of marital love.

If this fact is accepted, that the man is in a special way the reflection and representative of God and the woman is the reflection and representative of both creation and the church, then the biblical ordering of the sexes follows as a matter of course. We now understand that the man is called to leadership and sacrificial love in marriage and church, and that the woman is entrusted with submitting in love to the man. In being head the man expresses his special position as the representative of God, the head of creation and the church.

All this shows how deeply the biblical view of male and female is rooted in the nature of God. Whoever rejects the biblical ordering of the sexes must ultimately reject the God revealed in Holy Scripture. Feminist theologians are therefore only being consistent when they oppose not just the biblical ordering of the sexes but also the Bible's understanding of God.

As every consistent feminist theology must oppose the biblical view of God, a Christian feminist theology is impossible in itself. The American feminist Mary Daly has recognised this clearly in her book *Beyond God the Father*. In her foreword she writes that a feminist Christianity is just as much a self-contradiction as, say, the idea of a four-sided triangle.[447] 'There is no possibility of eliminating the male/masculine world of ideas from the word of God.'[448] For this reason Mary Daly has broken away from theological feminism.

The inseparable connection between the position of the sexes and the nature of God now helps us understand why Paul fights so keenly and uncompromisingly against any softening of the ordering of male and female. Paul realised that here central truths of the gospel were at stake.

After showing how the biblical view of the sexes is rooted in the nature of God, we can answer the question posed earlier (p. 63) whether the divine image in man covers his sexuality. On the basis of our discussions we can say to start with that the man reflects God in a special way by being a man, whereas the woman by being a woman is the reflection of creation. So up to a point the man may be said to reflect God or Christ more completely than the woman does,[449] whereas she more clearly portrays creation and the church[450] (*cf.* the parallels in Eph 5:22ff. Christ – husband, church – wife).[451] But this statement must not be misunderstood to mean that the woman is in only a limited sense the image of God. Genesis 1:27 ascribes without qualification God's image to both sexes. The statement about the image of God in man is a qualitative statement that permits no quantitative reduction. It means first of all that male and female by being human (*e.g.*, through their personality) reflect God, and that humanity is shared equally by both sexes. Only secondarily is it possible to differentiate slightly how man and woman reflect God through their sex. Here in the light of the total biblical witness obvious differences emerge which may be summed up by saying that the male reflects God in a special way and the female reflects creation. But this remark requires amplification if we are to do full justice to the biblical testimony.

We have already established (pp. 155–6) that God cannot be termed mother because the basic maternal functions of conception, pregnancy and birth, which are essentially passive in character, may not be ascribed to God without injuring his divinity. However, motherhood does not just consist in the primary biological functions just mentioned, but also in carrying out maternal activities such as the care of the weak and those in need of protection, the preservation of life and the careful upbringing of the child needing protection. In such activities the woman without doubt reflects God's caring, protective, and preserving love to his creatures. Through her particular ability of giving herself to others the woman can express God's personal love and devotion to the weak and needy in a way that comes more naturally to her than to men. This motherly side of God, which is of course part of his fatherliness (*cf*. pp. 156–7 above), is not just found in the God of Israel (Isa 66:13), but also in Jesus (Matt 23:37).

It has been correctly pointed out time and again that the 'motherly' side of God's nature is particularly obvious in the Holy Spirit. The Holy Spirit cares for the upbringing of the regenerate. They are compared in the New Testament to new-born children who must be carefully nursed, fed and brought up (*cf*. 1 Cor 3:1–2; Eph 4:13; 1 Pet 2:2; Heb 5:12–13). The Spirit appears as the comforter and advocate (*paraklētos*) of weak disciples in desperate situations (*cf*. Mark 13:11; John 14:16; Rom 8:26). This shows that in the activity of God's Spirit there are features which could be termed 'motherly'.

Can one then conclude, as some theologians do, that the Spirit of God is the female in God[452] or, as Zinzendorf says,[453] the 'mama' in the Trinity? These conclusions are totally inappropriate. If one contrasts the Holy Spirit as the 'female' in God with the 'male' Father and Son, a polarity is set up within the Trinity which conflicts with the identity of nature of the three divine persons. The Holy Spirit could never be described in Scripture as the bride of God the Father or the mother of Christ. Such concepts would be regarded by the biblical writers as pagan, for divine brides and mother goddesses are a feature of many non-Christian religions. The Holy Spirit is of the same nature as the Father and the Son, but the mode of his activity allows the 'motherly' nature of God special expression. However, the nature of the Holy Spirit contains nothing that is not also in the nature of the Father and the Son.

We have already seen that the 'motherly' aspect of God belongs to his fatherliness, which must be seen in much broader terms than human fatherliness. The 'motherly' activity of the Spirit is therefore God's nature being realised as a loving Father. All this shows that it is impossible to accept a difference of nature between a 'male' God the Father and a 'female' Spirit of God. None of the three divine persons of the Trinity can properly be characterised with female attributes so far as their essential nature is concerned.

The results of this section may be summed up in three statements:

1. The triune God revealed in Holy Scripture is not described in masculine categories by chance or for questionable patriarchal motives, but because God's nature cannot be properly portrayed otherwise.

2. The biblical view of God entails with consistent logic the headship of the man over the woman, for the man is in a special way the representative of the God revealed in Scripture.

3. Because the biblical ordering of the sexes is ultimately grounded in the nature of the living God, any attempt to interpret this ordering as culturally conditioned and in need of revision is bound to fail.

11

The Urgency of Practising the Biblical View of Man and Woman

There has been no period in history in which it was more urgent to put into practice the biblical view of male and female than today. For at present God's standards, and particularly the divine ordering of the sexes, are being questioned and set aside on a scale never experienced before. Our era is marked by the attempt to level out gender differences completely, or at least to reduce them to the undeniable physiological minima. This attempt has found its most radical expression in feminism, but it has affected the consciousness of many people of both sexes. This has led to a worrying loss of manliness and womanliness and to a deep uncertainty about what are the roles of men and women. Today whoever dares to use such terms as manliness and womanliness runs the risk of being laughed out of court as hopelessly backward. This of course is connected with the fact that in the past such terms were often used or abused quite thoughtlessly (think of the corruption of the manly ideal under the Third Reich!). But the main reason certainly lies in the modern rejection of a clearly defined picture of what it means to be male and female.

On the basis of our analysis we were able to produce a fairly precise picture of the particular characteristics of male and female from a biblical and anthropological perspective. If we now apply our results to examine our present situation, the following picture emerges.

1. Our age is suffering a serious loss of manliness. The term manliness in its biblical sense may be briefly defined as

the willingness to undertake leadership in a responsible and devoted fashion in marriage, family and society in accordance with God's standards. Judged by this picture of responsible manliness the present situation appears pretty dismal.

The flight from responsibility and the unwillingness to show devoted love towards women are apparent everywhere. More and more men refuse to give women life-long love and fidelity in marriage and the protection and security which the woman urgently needs. This is evident in the rapid growth of 'trial marriages' and the alarming rise in divorces in West Germany from 55,000 in 1964 to 108,000 in 1976. If men no longer give an unconditional 'yes' to marriage, it is no wonder that ever fewer women aspire to marry.

The loss of responsible manliness is also apparent in the ever-spreading flight from fatherhood. This flight from paternal responsibility shows itself on the one hand in an ever-declining willingness to give children the gift of life and on the other hand in the absence of paternal love and authority within family life. The flight from parenthood has already reached such a scale in West Germany that the future of our people is seriously threatened.[454] Currently West Germany has the lowest birthrate in the world. In addition there is a worrying loss of paternal responsibility in many families. In modern industrial society the man is often threatened with the loss of fatherly duties, of playing the role of the outsider even within his own family. This is partly because his career demands that he spend most of his day outside the home, partly because he deliberately cuts himself off from the family, and partly because his place and authority have been obscured by an all-too mechanical interpretation and application of the principle of equality, as if a society could consist entirely of equal brothers, without any fathers. That Holy Scripture calls 'being at home' 'being with his father'[455] should make us reconsider our attitudes.

It has been proved empirically that when fathers neglect their responsibilities there are destructive consequences for the whole family.[456] The flight of many men from their paternal responsibilities has led to many young people having to grow up without any examples to give them a sense of moral direction. There has grown up 'a fatherless society', a 'world without fathers'[457] which mistrusts any kind of authority, because it lacks the experience of a loving life-enhancing authority that comes from fathers. As a result a spiritual vacuum has arisen, a loss of direction and a purposelessness that has driven many young people to resignation, doubt, suicide, and destructive ideologies (Marxism, youth sects). And the so-called 'fatherless society' cannot dispense with the natural and therefore ineradicable need for fatherly authority and love. Even political movements which radically reject the existing authorities very soon raise up their own father figures (Marx, Lenin, Hitler, Mao, Che Guevara, *etc.*).

It is of decisive importance for a nation's life that its men are conscious of their responsibility and ready to dedicate themselves to being fathers, not just to delegate their educational role to their wives. Fatherhood comprises much more than merely biological procreation. Father 'in the full sense of the word is a man who has not just begotten a child, but one who is prepared to undertake as his responsibility the child's custody, provision and education, to be his provider, protector, carer and instructor'.[458] It can only be termed a tragedy that such a model has largely disappeared from human consciousness. A nation without fathers is a nation without a future!

With the loss of responsible manliness comes increased aggressiveness and with that more juvenile delinquency, which in West Germany and other Western countries is provoking growing anxiety. This aggressiveness is a type of ungoverned manliness, which runs aground by capitulating overhastily in the face of difficulties, and it is clearly connected with a deficient experience of parental security.

All the examples mentioned attest the regrettable loss of manliness in our society and the destructive consequences which follow. Today's lack of responsible maleness ultimately arises from the increasing rejection of God and his standards. Wherever a man no longer acknowledges God as his 'head', his own 'headship', and with it his manliness, must degenerate into a caricature that evokes rebellion against every kind of authority.[459] From this viewpoint we can understand the current trend towards levelling out the differences between the sexes, towards the emancipation of women as feminists understand it.

When the man is no longer prepared in sacrificial love to assume his responsibility in marriage, in family and in society, the woman is no longer ready to entrust herself to male leadership. The loss of masculinity therefore carries with it a loss of femininity. Male irresponsibility necessarily causes female irresponsibility: where the man no longer accepts his male tasks, the woman also rebels against her tasks. It is just this development that we can observe so clearly today.

2. We do not have just a 'fatherless society', but also increasingly a 'motherless society', as ever fewer women are ready to carry out their tasks as mothers with total commitment. We do not just have men rebelling against life-long marriage, but also increasingly the reluctance of women to bind themselves for ever to one husband. A pointer in this direction is that according to a West German opinion poll in 1973 only 2% of unmarried women between nineteen and twenty-nine years old held that it was going too far to live with a man without marrying him. Whereas in 1967 65% still opposed this idea. If men are not worthy of trust, it is no surprise if women refuse to trust them.

At bottom feminism is the consistent unloving answer to men's lack of love! Feminist ideology, which in dogged onesidedness reflects the interests of the woman without considering with equal seriousness the interests of the man, is an understandable reaction to the ruthlessness with which men have often propagated their interests. The tragedy of feminism is that it propagates precisely the opposite of the real interests of women. Instead of helping women to develop their femaleness to its optimum, it tends to encourage them to imitate men. Women should participate to the same extent as men in careers, in society, and in politics. The 'masculinisation' of women that goes with this is bought at the cost of a radical devaluation of the most vital maternal tasks. The standard for feminist demands is paradoxically what *men* do, and not what corresponds to a woman's nature.

The price which women must pay for this is the loss of their femininity. 'Woman becomes a caricature, a pseudo-being.'[460] Since feminism in effect works towards the destruction of femaleness, it proves to be a movement extremely hostile towards women! This knowledge has led a former feminist to make this provocative remark: 'The great historical disaster for women is the idea of emancipation.'[461] The mistake, of course, does not lie in the idea of emancipation as such, but in a misunderstanding of emancipation. 'True emancipation of women should not attempt to stop the woman from being herself or take her away from what is intrinsically hers.'[462] What today usually passes for the emancipation of women tends, despite many justified demands (*e.g.*, against pornography and rape) towards the abolition of the female.

The process of the increasing masculinisation of women has long been in full swing. As men widely deny their God-given tasks, so many women rebel against their position in creation, which is to be the man's support and to be mothers. This is seen, for example, in today's widespread devaluation of those who are 'just housewives', and of mothers who do not pursue a career. For many women at any rate a career is only an escape, which indicates that they still have not been able to give a total 'yes' to their life as wife and mother. Instead they seek fulfilment outside the family. As long as one inwardly revolts against a task, this task becomes a necessary burden rather than a source of joy. The problem for many women arises from the fact that their sacrificial task of motherhood is not properly recognised by their husbands. Consequently it becomes unnecessarily difficult for them joyfully to accept motherhood and those household chores which, as T. Friedmann says, are an extension of motherhood.[463]

Furthermore, motherhood for a long time has not received from public opinion the valuation that it merits. Today's intellectual climate makes it tremendously difficult for the

woman to affirm unreservedly her femaleness and her tasks as
wife and mother. One of the shocking consequences is that as
a result of following their career many women badly neglect
their maternal duties. The damage to children and society
that this causes is incalculably high.[464] The decline in
maternal responsibility and readiness to sacrifice is probably
the most regrettable result of the loss of femininity which
characterises the present. The loss of femininity in society,
like the loss of masculinity described earlier, carries with it
similarly destructive results. When a nation has no clear
model in which the special tasks of men and women, fathers
and mothers are displayed, then the foundations of national
life are threatened. A nation needs not just a sharply defined
image of what it means to be human, but also a clear picture of
what it means to be male or female.

Holy Scripture does not let us down at this point, but
mediates valid truth about people and about the sexes. The
biblical view of male and female is burningly relevant today.
It is the task of Christendom to put this biblical view of the
sexes into practice and to live it out, showing to the puzzled
world what it means to be a man or a woman as God intended.
The church of Christ is commissioned, as 'a city set on a hill'
and 'the light of the world' (Matt 5:14–15), to make it clear
that God's creation ordinance for man and woman enhances
life and cannot be set aside without detriment. The church of
Jesus Christ should be a model showing how the sexes may
live together harmoniously, a model in which both male
and female develop their own character and beautifully
complement each other.

If the present situation in Christianity is looked at soberly,
it must be admitted that among Christians too there is great
uncertainty about God's intentions for the sexes. Even
committed Christians, who want to hold on to the authority of
Scripture for doctrine and practice, tend to question the
abiding validity of the biblical ordering of male and female.
On the other hand there are conservative Christians who
interpret the biblical view to the woman's disadvantage, so
failing to recognise that the Bible sharply condemns the

egoism of both sexes and calls them both similarly to repentance.

All this shows that Christendom urgently needs an inner renewal in order to live credibly before the world, as it puts into practice the divine creator's purpose for men and women to live together. The church needs above all a passionate new attachment to the will of God, a one-sided devotion to God alone and a comprehensive rejection of the spirit of the world. This recognition of God's lordship is urgently needed and intrinsically involves affirming and putting into practice the divine ordering of the sexes. A Christianity which refuses to obey God at this point risks its power, for a disobedient Christianity guided by the spirit of the age attracts the wrath and judgement of God. A real and lasting spiritual renewal of the church of Jesus Christ cannot occur if the divine ordering of male and female is disregarded.

In what follows we want to show what practical consequences flow from this knowledge.

1. The very first requirement is that Christians should once again reflect on the biblical view of male and female. Then they will rediscover what a rich understanding the biblical view contains and what blessing rests on its practice. What it means to be a man under the lordship of Christ seems to me a question of particular importance. This question has largely been neglected by Christians. Though there is much good literature, especially Catholic works,[465] about the Christian woman, there is little about the Christian man.

Perhaps the best book on this topic is the splendid, though sadly barely known, work by the Catholic theologian Heinrich David, *The Image of the Christian Man*. His presentation combines theological depth with helpful practical discussions (including discussion of the single life), and can be most warmly recommended.

The neglect of this question of the Christian man has severely damaged Christianity and contributed to many more men than women turning their backs on the gospel. This is obviously because the preaching does not address their maleness sufficiently. Many men feel that piety is something for old ladies and children. Certainly this attitude is also connected with the presumptuous pride of many men, who do not want to submit totally to another master. But male pride by itself cannot suffice to explain the widespread feminisation of the church. There are good reasons to suppose that the church's preaching has overstressed the comfort of the gospel and has failed to emphasise that we are conscripted by Christ to build the kingdom. It is the latter that appeals to man's nature, which is geared to action and change. The passive side of faith, the acceptance of peace and security through the forgiveness of sins, has often been overstressed at the cost of the active side of faith, the renewal of human thought, will and action through the Holy Spirit. If preaching offers male activism no scope for action, it is no surprise if it does not reach many men. A sermon restricted to pious spirituality and introspection will pass most men by. It also falls well below the level of the New Testament. The spiritual emigration of men out of the church poses a serious challenge to the reality of ecclesiastical preaching and theology. Men who must live out their daily lives in the often hard world of work will not be touched by pious thoughts or feelings by themselves, but be convinced only by experiencing the reality of God.

The alienation of many men from the gospel and the church is not just a problem for the preacher, but more precisely for the theologian, for the quality of the theology determines the quality of preaching. The unreality which characterises some twentieth-century theology[466] is in fair measure to blame for the unreality of church practice. Only a decisive return to the teaching of the New Testament will give theology and church practice the revolutionary power which characterised first-century Christianity and enable the church to appeal to men. The decline in church attendance by many men shows us very clearly how urgent it is to explore the peculiarly male aspect of Christian discipleship.

The Bible contains much more material on this question than can be tackled in this book. Just an examination of some of the men in the Bible could contribute much to building an image of the Christian man. Similarly a study of the women of the Bible could contribute something decisive to a Christian image of women. For example, a comparison of Abraham, the father of the faithful (*cf*. Gal 3:7), with Mary, the mother of the faithful, could yield profound insights into male and female expressions of faith. Whereas Abraham's faith is active and expansive (migrating to Canaan, offering Isaac, *etc*.), Mary's faith consists completely in receiving, in letting happen what God is doing within her (*cf*. Luke 1:38: '. . . let it be to me according to your word'). Mary is certainly the most important woman in Scripture if one wants to see what it means to be female and to follow Christ. It has been a spiritual loss to Protestantism that Mary is hardly honoured as the unique model of a woman who has faith in Christ.[467] This is despite the fact that Luther in his 'Magnificat' beautifully depicts the exemplariness of the mother of Christ. Even if Catholic authors sometimes overvalue Mary, Protestants may well learn something important from Catholic presentations of her.

Christian consideration of the biblical view of male and female is necessary and may help the rediscovery and understanding of some central Christian truths. Often lurking behind the rejection of the biblical ordering of the sexes lies a rejection of central truths of the gospel. Behind many Christians' rejection of the subordination of women to men lies a fundamental reluctance to obey any human being. This mistrust receives apparent spiritual support from the call to obey God alone. That obedience towards God often in practice simply means obeying other people (parents, those in authority, state, church, pastors, *etc*.) is thereby overlooked. Obedience according to the New Testament is not at all demeaning. The Son of God not only obeyed his Father in everything, but also his earthly parents for a long time (*cf*. Luke 2:51). Since in our age authority and obedience have been largely put in question, many Christians find it difficult to grasp that among the fundamentals of the gospel 'obedience is to be valued as our highest and most noble achievement'.[468] The Swiss saint Nicholas von der Flue could thus write to the Council of Bern: 'Obedience is the greatest honour that there is in heaven or earth; so you must endeavour to be obedient to each other.'[469] In the face of the anti-authoritarian ideologies of our time, it would be a great gain if Christians could credibly demonstrate how obedience in love and freedom for God's sake is indispensable for mankind. Christian couples and families are specially suited to demonstrating this convincingly.

2. The biblical ordering of man and woman is preserved by Christendom only if it assumes visible form in the ordering of church life. This means that the offices of pastor and teacher may not be taken over by women without deserting the biblical view of the sexes. The unrestricted pastoral office allowed women in many Protestant churches is therefore untenable. This has already become sufficiently clear from our earlier discussion (cf. especially Chapter 10). Nevertheless, we want to sum up briefly in an excursus the real reasons against allowing women to become parish priests.

Excursus 5
Why a female priesthood is theologically untenable

First two introductory points:

1. This excursus presupposes Chapters 5 to 9 and builds on their conclusions. For a fuller understanding of the reasons given here these chapters must be consulted.

2. The following discussion is concerned only with the question whether it is theologically responsible to have women clergy in charge of a church, not with the question whether a woman may be a minister in special situations (e.g., as a hospital or prison chaplain to women).

Women clergy in charge of churches must be rejected for the following theological reasons:

1. The New Testament excludes women from exercising a teaching or leadership office within the church (1 Cor 14:33–5; 1 Tim 2:12). Both passages base their approach not on superficial pragmatic reasons, but on important and fundamental theological ones.

2. The New Testament's denial of church leadership to women is

indirectly supported by (a) the Old Testament permitting only male priests, and (b) the New Testament mentioning only male apostles and church leaders. Thus both the Old and New Testament church entrusted its spiritual leadership entirely to men.

3. The New Testament's denial of leadership offices to women arises necessarily out of the total biblical picture of male and female. Since in Scripture the man is placed over the woman because of the divine creation ordinance, women cannot exercise church leadership without setting aside male headship and thereby coming into conflict with the creator's will and their God-given nature as women. Saying 'yes' to spiritual leadership by women would according to biblical conviction be saying 'no' to God's creation and therefore be rebellion against God himself; the redemption in Christ does not nullify the creation arrangements. Since the Bible inextricably links together its total outlook on the sexes and its rejection of women as church leaders, it necessarily follows that those who accept women as parish priests must, if they are consistent, give up the biblical ordering of male and female (that is male headship).

4. Scripture's rejection of women as priests and church leaders is not derived from its patriarchally oriented contemporary culture, but rests on God's revelation in Israel and in Christ. Biblical practice stands in striking contradiction to the practice of the ancient Orient and the classical world. It claims rather to rest on the instructions of Yahweh (Lev 21) and the example of Jesus, who called only male apostles (Matt 10:1–4 and parallels).

5. The most profound reason for the Bible's 'no' to a female priesthood and church leadership arises from the nature of the living God. The apostles and New Testament church leaders, just like the Old Testament priests, had the task of being God's representatives (see above pp. 152–3). In certain respects (namely in his essential nature as creator and father), the God revealed in Holy Scripture can be represented only by the male. Because God is *Father*, Jesus is God's *Son* begotten of the same nature. Because Jesus was *a man*, only male apostles and church leaders can represent him. Since it is of the essence of the office of church pastor to represent Christ as the pastor of the church, it is intrinsically impossible for the office of parish priest to be filled by a woman.

6. It is not just biblical revelation, including its doctrine of God, that is against women as parish clergy, but two thousand years of

ecumenical Christian tradition. Protestants, Catholics and Orthodox have up to our century unanimously maintained that the
pastoral office should be restricted to men. Protestant retreat from
this practice happened in clear contradiction to Luther[470] and has
irresponsibly deepened the division in Christianity. Church renewal
in which no account is taken of the totality of Christ's body and its
divinely intended unity (cf. John 17:21; Eph 4:3–13) cannot be
spiritual. The Protestant departure from hitherto ecumenical
practice is the more regrettable as the tradition accepted hitherto
rests on Holy Scripture, whereas admitting women to the pastoral
office is an aberration of fanatical and heretical movements such as
Montanism and Gnosticism.

7. Finally, two insights into the nature of male and female also
militate against allowing women to become parish priests. There
are plenty of observations showing that the man is normally more
suited to leadership than the woman is (cf. above pp. 37–8 and
147).[471] However, one must beware of basing too much on
psychological insights and pragmatic considerations (e.g., the
difficulties women clergy face in marriage and motherhood), for the
decisive reasons against them are theological in nature.

These reasons show sufficiently that a female priesthood cannot
be justified theologically. It can only be very much hoped that those
churches which have not opened their pastoral office to women will
maintain their fidelity to the Lord of the church and encourage
other churches to retreat from their irresponsible decision.

Our discussion does not immediately affect those particular
functions of clergywomen which do not involve church leadership
(e.g., pastoral work in hospitals or women's prisons). There is no
objection to women undertaking these kinds of service. Really it is
the concept of a woman vicar or rector that causes problems, for
such offices involve church leadership. It would be better for
women who undertake pastoral duties which do not involve leading
the church to be part of an extended order of deaconesses or a
special order of assistant women curates.

Finally we must tackle a widespread misunderstanding. It is
maintained again and again that the exclusion of women from the
priesthood is discriminatory, for they are being refused a right that
is allowed to men. In reply it must be said that the office of pastor in
the church of Jesus Christ is not a general human right (not even for
men), but that it represents a special divine calling of a minority of
believers. Neither being male nor believing in Christ qualifies

someone to be a pastor in the church, only God's inner call and an outward commissioning by the church. Whoever regards not being called to a pastoral or teaching office as discriminatory has missed the fact that spiritual office within the church is an unearned gift of God.

Another fatal misunderstanding of the New Testament's denial of the pastoral (priestly) office to women is to suppose that it reflects a devaluation of women. It is precisely the opposite. It is because the New Testament unconditionally affirms the character and value of femaleness that it opposes women being pastors, for this is incompatible with their true nature. Putting it another way, God does not commission women to be leaders in his church, because he has entrusted them with other tasks compatible with their nature in which their femaleness can be fully developed. As Schlatter observes, the New Testament 'contains no dictatorial word, no word which is not meant to minister to us'.[472] This applies to its refusal to allow women pastors.

The frequently made observation that God has blessed the ministry of women clergy is not a valid argument for ordaining them to the priesthood. For God's mercy is so great that he often blesses human ministry despite disobedience or error. It is also very problematic to appeal to human experience against the clear statements of Holy Scripture.

Does the theological untenability of women priests mean that women are barred from any form of preaching ministry? The answer is obviously 'no'. If there were prophetesses in ancient Israel and in the New Testament church, even if not active in public worship, that at least shows prophetic preaching by women has biblical justification. The New Testament also explicitly endorses the instruction of women and children by women (cf. Tit 2:3–4; 2 Tim 1:5; 3:15). From that we conclude that the ministry of catechesis and preaching is spiritually legitimate for women within certain limits.

But what are these limits? The New Testament lays down two quite clear boundaries which may not be transgressed.

1. The offices of authoritative instruction and church

leadership are fundamentally limited to men, both in individual churches and in the universal church.

2. The office of preaching is only legitimate where it is endowed and commissioned by the Holy Spirit. In the New Testament this applies to both sexes. Everything a Christian does must be 'in the Lord' or 'in the Spirit' (*e.g.*, Col 3:17).

Church history provides many examples of women who have preached the gospel without thereby putting in question the male office of teacher or church leader. The preaching ministry of Hildegard of Bingen or Catherine of Siena in the Middle Ages, or Dora Rappard or Sister Eva of Tiele-Winckler, can as little be called in spiritual question as, for example, the richly blessed ministry of the Dutchwoman Corrie ten Boom or the sacrificial work of many women missionaries. To reject such ministries would be to quench the Spirit. But to question the exclusively male pastoral and teaching office on the basis of such ministries would be a failure to recognise the divinely intended ordering of the sexes.[473]

The church of Jesus Christ must always be concerned that both God's creation ordinances and the activity of the Holy Spirit must receive their rightful place, knowing that there is never a real conflict between them. To despise the created order is to forfeit any claim to inspiration by the Holy Spirit. Of course there are exceptional situations (*e.g.*, on the mission field or in war time where there is no man available) where a woman must temporarily take on the functions of church leadership. But it is vital, if a woman's ministry is to be spiritually acceptable in such circumstances, that both she and the church recognise the provisional and proxy character of her ministry and that no permanent pastoral office develops from it.

The biblical ordering of male and female must be visibly accepted at every level of church life. In practice this means that in all mixed Christian groups and circles the headship of the male should be expressed, that men should assume the task of leadership and direction. This principle is also valid in housegroups. In unusual circumstances it can of course be spiritually legitimate to allow a woman to run a housegroup as an interim solution until God provides a man. But there is nothing problematic about allowing a woman to fulfil the task of spiritual leader where she is dealing with women (*e.g.*, in wives' or Mothers' Union groups) or with children of both sexes (*e.g.*, in children's worship or religious instruction).

3. Decisively important for the Christian renewal of the church is the spiritual renewal of Christian marriages and families. When the divine ordering of man and woman, as it is described in Ephesians 5:22ff., takes shape in the marriages of Christians, Christian churches will blossom in an unanticipated way and experience God's blessing. The divine life developing in marriages and families will stream out into the churches and heal church life.

Without spiritually convincing marriages there are no spiritually convincing churches. If men and women do not succeed in living together in marriage, they will also fail in church life. But the more convincingly husbands reflect Jesus' treatment of the church in the sense of Ephesians 5:22ff., and Christian fathers mirror God's loving fatherhood, the more credible will the love of God be to people around them. Christian marriages and Christian churches in which the biblical ordering of male and female takes shape offer a unique acted parable of the eternal love of the triune God.

A sober look at modern Christendom shows that many Christian marriages and families do not take seriously the New Testament ordering of marriage. Whereas previously too many Christian men fell into the trap of justifying their authoritarian domination of wife and family because they were head, today there is the opposite danger: Christian husbands, either for a quiet life or by wrongly adapting to the spirit of the age, are not ready to assume their position as head. Many Christian fathers, for example, deny their headship by leaving the spiritual upbringing of their children entirely to their wives and by so doing renege on their great responsibility to be spiritual head of the family. We all ought to pay attention to Heinrich David's earnest exhortation.

As the head of the family, the father should be the first to arrange for the correct religious instruction and further upbringing of his family; he should be the first to pray and sacrifice with and for his family; he should be the first to exercise the right and duty to bless them; he should be the first involved in the various decisions and measures to develop the spiritual life of the child . . . In a special way he and his own example should kindle the religious life of the family. He is teacher, priest and pastor of the family, or as Augustine put it, he is bishop of the family.[474]

When Christian husbands put their headship into practice in this way, they fulfil their maleness in the way that God intended. Fulfilling the headship that the New Testament envisaged involves the man in a school of selflessness and love, in which he has daily opportunity to crucify his male egoism. Correspondingly, Christian women in their marriages have ample opportunities as wives and mothers to live for others and to sacrifice everything that hinders them from being unconditionally their husband's partner and their children's mother. Sadly, it must be said at this point that many Christian women are not prepared to realise with total consistency their nature and to be their husband's helpmeets and mothers as God intended. More and more are influenced by the spirit of the age and rebel against the man's headship and the total demand of being a mother.

Everywhere we see a tendency to level out the differences between the sexes, a tendency that is contrary to creation. A rejection of every kind of order or subordination has not passed the Christian world by either. Particularly among young Christians there is a rejection of the biblical ordering of male and female, or at least a deep uncertainty about the God-appointed tasks of the sexes. In this situation men and women are called to repent, to reflect afresh on the ordering of the sexes revealed in Holy Scripture, and with total earnestness to put it into practice. This means both sexes should clearly refuse all attempts at self-fulfilment which deny or endanger the divine vocation of male and female. Instead of personal self-fulfilment men and women are called to a higher goal. They are called to reflect in marriage the sacrificial divine love through mutual devotion to each other – to be a witness to a world which has taught itself not to believe in the love of God.

12

Summary of Main Points and Conclusions

1. The biblical view of the sexes can be summed up in three points:
   a. The unconditional affirmation of sexuality within divinely set boundaries as a good creation of God.
   b. The full equality of man and woman because both were made in God's image and fully redeemed in Christ.
   c. The distinction of male and female, which involves different tasks for the sexes and a different position of man and woman.
2. The biblical ordering of the sexes consists in the man being seen as the head of the woman and the woman as supporter of the man (Gen 2).
3. Headship for the man means:
   a. The task of leadership and direction in marriage, church and society.
   b. The acceptance of this leadership in dedicated selfless love, imitating Christ.
4. The position of supporter for the woman means:
   a. Loving subordination under male leadership.
   b. Completing the man by her special gifts as a woman.
5. The biblical ordering of man and woman (male superordination and female subordination) is an ordering in love, is sanctified by love and is also limited by it.
   a. It is sanctified by love in that it reflects the eternal, inner-trinitarian love of God (1 Cor 11:3) and the covenant of love between Christ and the church (Eph 5:22ff.).

    b. It is limited by love, since love makes impossible every type of arbitrary male despotism and every slavish subjection of women.

6. As an ordinance of creation the biblical ordering of man and woman fundamentally applies to everyone, since it rests on the created nature of male and female.

7. As an ordinance of total love it presupposes the new person who has been redeemed in Christ and in him freed from egoism for selflessness.

8. As an ordinance of selfless love it ends the age-old battle of the sexes; it brings both sexes to God's intended development of their character, and so fulfils God's creative intention for male and female.

9. The biblical view of the sexes is the perpetually valid Christian answer to the perversion of masculinity and femininity by unredeemed humanity. It is a call to repentance directed at both sexes which condemns both the oppression and devaluation of women just as much as the feminist revolt against God's creation ordinance.

10. The biblical view of the sexes is of peculiar relevance to the present, for never before have the fundamental differences between men and women been so denied and the levelling out of all, except physiological, gender differences been so propagated. Behind this tendency to identify the sexes with each other, which finds its sharpest ideological expression in feminism, lies the confusion of the equality of the sexes with their identity. From the viewpoint of biblical theology this tendency is ultimately an anti-Christian rebellion against the divinely intended destiny of male and female. It must be seen as part of the eschatological rebellion of autonomous man against God's ordinances and commands. That feminism is ultimately anti-Christian is frankly admitted by the feminist Mary Daly: 'In its depth, because it contains a dynamic that drives beyond Christolatry [*i.e.*, the worship of Christ], the women's movement *does* point to, seek and constitute the primordial, always present, and future Antichrist.'[475]

11. Currently fashionable attempts to relativise the biblical

view of man and woman as culturally conditioned and in need of revision are bound to founder. This is because the biblical view of the sexes is characteristically different from the conceptions of its contemporary environment.

12. A more precise analysis of the biblical view of the sexes shows that it is not only based on the created nature of man and woman, but ultimately on the nature of God himself. This means that a rejection of this view affects the Christian view of God and with it the fundamentals of the Christian faith and Christian theology.

13. The Christian church should therefore make it one of its central tasks to put into practice the biblical view of man and woman as fully and consistently as possible.

14. An unavoidable consequence of the biblical ordering of the sexes is the rejection of a female priesthood.

15. The spiritual power and authority of Christianity depends on making the biblical view of man and woman a reality. A spiritual renewal of the church of Jesus Christ can only be permanently effective if the biblical view of the sexes is recognised as a valid norm for Christian marriage and for the church.

Notes

For full details of the publications cited here, see the Bibliography. Where there is more than one work by an author, the date of publication is cited.

1 Kühlwetter, Offenberg and Moltmann-Wendel (1977), 33–54, provide a short survey of the history of the women's movement. Menschick has a good collection of source material. Höhler and Janowski have good introductions to the newer feminism. Among female critics of feminism, see the clever and concerned books of the Greek A. Stassinopoulos, the Swede, M. Scherer, and the German sociologist, U. Erler.
2 de Beauvoir, 273.
3 *cf. ibid.*, 673–87.
4 *cf. ibid.*, 142, 474, 656.
5 *ibid.*, 467–74.
6 Firestone, 1–13.
7 *Ibid.*, 223–4, 233.
8 *Ibid.*, 223, 261–2.
9 *Ibid.*, 2.
10 *Ibid.*, 1.
11 Schwarzer, 205. According to her (*ibid.*, 206), sexual intercourse is an intrinsically violent act of a man against a woman.
12 *e.g., ibid.*, 192. According to Schwarzer (*ibid.*, 193), the sole surviving difference between the sexes is that women can give birth.
13 *cf.* Sullerot, 594; Kuehneldt-Leddihn (1975), 36f.
14 *cf.* Goldberg, 25–8, 37–47; Tiger, 12.
15 Schrey and Moltmann-Wendel (1977) offer an introductory survey of theological feminism.
16 On this, see Moltmann-Wendel (1979), 341.
17 *cf.* Röper, 84; Moltmann-Wendel (1979), 342; Mayr, 250–5. At the World Missionary Conference in Melbourne in May 1980 an American

delegate went so far as to propose that 'prayer to God as father be eliminated, since this title of God was sexist, describing him as a male being' (*cf. Spektrum* 23 (1980), 1).

18 *cf.* Russell.

19 Swidler.

20 Moltmann-Wendel (1979), 341. Since then two more conferences on feminist theology have taken place at Bad Boll. For reports on the three conferences and an insight into church feminism in West Germany, see Kahl, *et al. Feministische Theologie-Praxis* (1981). A careful reading of this book must profoundly shock any Christian who upholds the Scriptures. This feminist theology does not just remodel the Christian doctrine of God in a heretical way, but alters other central Christian doctrines such as the atonement, justification, sin, and the doctrine of Scripture.

21 For example, at the 1979 Evangelischer Kirchentag in Nuremberg feminists mounted a blasphemous display of a crucified woman with the caption '1979 years of Church against Women' (*Reutlinger General Anzeiger*, 16 June 1979, 18).

22 Fundamentally no ethic can have a firm foundation without the knowledge that there is a personal God, as every ethic stands or falls by the assumption of an absolute distinction between good and evil. If there is no personal God this assumption is ultimately unprovable and without binding authority, being merely a human supposition. But if a real personal God exists, then there is an absolute distinction between good and evil based on God's nature and commands. The ethical judgement that both sexes are equal merely remains a postulate if one does not begin with the existence of a personal God.

23 *cf.* Kampmann, I, 87f. (on Schopenhauer), 86f. (on Nietzsche), 87f. (on Kant). Stopczyk gives an interesting survey of the evaluation of women in the history of philosophy.

24 *cf.* Kampmann, I, 79f.

25 *cf.* Weininger, 220–60. Weininger (220) goes so far as to maintain that the 'lowest man is infinitely higher than the highest woman'.

26 *cf.* Lersch, 126.

27 By soul I understand the seat of thought, will and feeling in a human being, which makes possible psychological, intellectual, moral and religious life. Through the soul a human being becomes a person.

28 On the sexuality of the human soul, *cf.* Zimmermann, 104–12.

29 For example, it is confirmed by research in psychosomatic medicine.

30 *cf.* Tresmontant, 98–105. For example, the unitary view of man in the Bible is apparent in that the key anthropological concepts of 'heart', 'soul', 'flesh', and 'spirit' describe not just particular aspects of human existence, but can designate the whole human being (Wolff, 7).

31 Leist (1970), 33.

32 *ibid.*, 37.

33 Metzke, 213.
34 *cf.* Bailey, 19–60.
35 *cf.* Lersch, 32f.; Kampmann, II, 227f.
36 *cf.* Lersch, 34; Kampmann, II, 167ff., 354, and our discussion on pp. 46–9.
37 Lück, 29–39, offers a good description and analysis of role theory. Our excursus relies heavily on him, except for the particular issue of sexual roles, which Lück only mentions in passing (*ibid.*, 34f.).
38 Ev. Erwachsenenkatechismus, 465.
39 *cf.* Dahrendorf, 70–88.
40 For a preliminary survey the following are recommended: Meves (1977b), Eysenck, 201–11, Huber, von Kuehneldt-Leddhin (1975), 36–84, 237–71, Stassinopoulos, 22–40, and Ziegler, 245–63. For more thorough discussion, see the large studies by Kampmann, Buytendijk, Lersch, Goldberg, Hutt and Sullerot.
41 Our description of the primary and secondary gender differences depends on Lersch, 24–37.
42 Rötzer, 7.
43 Leist (1970), 33.
44 Baader, XI, 75; *cf.* p. 128: 'Everything external about things may be viewed as a sign of what they are like internally.'
45 Modern biology in my opinion tends in this direction (*cf.* the useful analysis and criticism by the biologist W. Kuhn). The untenability of this view, which contests the qualitative difference between man and the animals, has been convincingly demonstrated biologically by Adolph Portmann in his pioneering work on the biological uniqueness of man.
46 Heitler, 83.
47 Lersch, 24.
48 *ibid.*
49 *ibid.*, 31. On the differences in bone structure see Kampmann, I, 171ff.
50 Lersch, 31.
51 Eckstein, 270.
52 *ibid.*
53 Lersch, 32.
54 *ibid.*
55 H. Sellheim, *Das Geheimnis vom Ewig-Weiblichen*, 206, quoted by Kampmann, I, 164.
56 C. Hoenig-Sidersleben, 'Die Ableitung der seelischen Geschlechts-unterschiede aus Trieben und Instinkten,' *Monatsschrift für Psychologie und Neurologie* 56 (1924), 361, quoted by Kampmann, I, 165.
57 Buytendijk, 104.
58 Lersch, 32.
59 *ibid.*, 26.
60 *ibid.*, 33. *Cf.* Kampmann, I, 167ff., on women's skin.

61 Lersch, 34. *Cf*. Kampmann, II, 167ff., 354, on female empathy.
62 Buytendijk, 279. *Cf*. Sullerot, 228.
63 On psychological motherhood, *cf*. Kampmann, II, 80–94; Buytendijk, 278–90.
64 Kampmann, II, 88.
65 *ibid*.
66 *cf. ibid*., 56ff.; Buytendijk, 117; Sullerot, 316.
67 Kampmann, II, 58.
68 *ibid*.
69 Stern, 286.
70 Lersch, 26.
71 *ibid*.
72 Kampmann, II, 66.
73 *ibid*., 66–8.
74 *cf*. Kampmann, II, 55ff.; Sullerot, 315.
75 *cf*. Eysenck, 203f; Kampmann, II, 55f., 105ff.; Meves (1977b), 24ff.
76 *cf*. Goldberg, 63–117; Eysenck, 204f.
77 *cf*. Eysenck, 208; Kaltenbrunner, 11f.; Goldberg, 179–85; Hutt, 98–105; Meves (1977b), 23f.
78 *cf*. Kampmann, II, 67; Eysenck, 209.
79 *cf*. Sullerot, 317.
80 *cf*. Kampmann, II, 67.
81 *cf*. Sullerot, 342; Eysenck, 209.
82 *cf*. Kampmann, II, 167ff., 181f., 354f.; Lersch, 34.
83 Lersch, 26f. *Cf*. Meves (1977b), 23: 'The male sex is programmed towards achievement [*i.e.*, getting things done], expansion, and change: it is women who have the sense to arrange what has been achieved!'
84 *cf*. Kampmann, I, 174; Sullerot, 238, 198.
85 *cf*. Kampmann, I, 130–6; Sullerot, 244.
86 Kampmann, I, 133; *cf. ibid*., 151f.
87 *ibid*., 133f.; *cf*. Sullerot, 244.
88 *cf*. Portmann, 57–61.
89 Chromosomes carry the genes (the basis of inheritance).
90 Lenz quoted from Kampmann, I, 127 (emphasis Neuer's).
91 *cf*. Goldberg, 87ff.; Sullerot, 369ff.
92 *cf*. Kampmann, I, 161ff.
93 *cf. ibid*., 155ff.
94 *cf. ibid*., 159ff.
95 *cf*. Witelson, Restak, and our discussion on p. 54.
96 *cf*. Baulieu and Haeur, 179; *Frankfurter Allgemeine Zeitung*, 152 (4 July 1979), 25.
97 *cf*. Lersch, 97f. For example, men have some female hormones just as women have some male hormones (*cf*. Baulieu and Haeur, 156–61). Thus it may be said 'that every organism is bisexual to some degree' (Clara, 25).

98 Meves (1977b), 21f.
99 *ibid.*, 22.
100 Zazzo, 312f. *Cf.* Witelson, 342f.
101 Zazzo, 314.
102 Witelson, 342.
103 *ibid.*, 342ff.
104 Sullerot, 334.
105 Goldberg, 167.
106 Eysenck, 208.
107 Sullerot, 337; Hutt, 89f.; Hofstätter, 135; Eysenck, 208.
108 *cf.* Goldberg, 179–85; Kaltenbrunner, 11f.
109 Eberhard, 50. The figures come from the period before 1927. Despite enquiry at the German patent office in Munich, I have not been able to obtain more recent figures. However, an official at the German patent office confirmed to me that even today the overwhelming number of individual inventions are made by men.
110 Eysenck, 209.
111 *ibid. Cf.* Hutt, 98–105.
112 Reidick, 83.
113 von le Fort, 128f.
114 Reidick, 83.
115 von le Fort, 129f.
116 *cf.* Kampmann, II, 293–317; Lersch, 62ff.; von Kuehneldt-Leddihn (1975), 58f.
117 Kampmann, II, 178, 293; Lersch, 70–8.
118 *cf.* Lersch, 70ff.
119 *ibid.*, 65.
120 Witelson, 358.
121 *ibid.*
122 *cf.* Lersch, 88; Kampmann, II, 31, 94f.; 159ff.
123 Lersch, 56.
124 Kampmann, II, 159.
125 *ibid.*, 127–224; Eysenck, 202f.
126 Kampmann, II, 161.
127 *ibid.*
128 *ibid.*
129 *ibid.*, 166.
130 *cf.* Lersch, 33.
131 Kampmann, II, 163.
132 *cf. ibid.*, 131–7.
133 *ibid.*, 167ff.
134 *ibid.*, 169.
135 E. Croner, *Die Frauenseele in den Übergangsjahren*, Langensalza, 1928, 41, quoted by Kampmann, II, 169.
136 *ibid.*

137 Kampmann, II, 170.
138 Scheler, 29.
139 Eysenck, 207. *Cf.* Kampmann, II, 59ff., 83ff., 95f.
140 Eysenck, 206.
141 Zazzo, 317.
142 *cf.* Eysenck, 205f.
143 Goldberg, 37–44.
144 *ibid.*, 87–92, 97f.
145 *cf.* Huber, 74ff.
146 Eysenck, 203f.
147 *cf.*, besides Kampmann, also Schmidtchen, 10–19.
148 Kampmann, II, 58f., 78.
149 *ibid.*, 59.
150 *ibid.*, 206f.
151 Lippert, *Die weibliche Vorpubertät im Spiegel des Backfischbuches*, Erfurt, ²1934, 50, quoted by Kampmann, II, 208.
152 Lippert, *op. cit.*, 88, quoted by Kampmann, II, 208.
153 *ibid.*
154 *ibid.*, 208f.
155 Huth, *Beiträge zur Untersuchung der seelischen Geschlechtsunterschiede im vorschulpflichtigen Alter*, Langensalza, 1926, 13, quoted by Kampmann, II, 210f.
156 Huth, *op. cit.*, 79 in Kampmann, II, 197.
157 Kampmann, II, 203.
158 Kerschensteiner, *Theorie der Bildung*, Leipzig and Berlin, 1926, 286, quoted by Kampmann, II, 203.
159 *cf.* M. Mead's book, *Male and Female*, London, 1949.
160 *cf.* Witelson; Restak; Stassinopoulos, 32; von Kuehneldt-Leddihn (1977), 36f.
161 *cf.* Witelson, 350, 356ff.
162 Witelson, 345; *cf.* Goldberg, 172.
163 Kampmann, II, 315.
164 *ibid.*, 316.
165 *ibid.*
166 *cf.* Witelson, 345; *cf.* Zander, 62.
167 *cf.* Goldberg, 87–94; Eysenck, 203f.
168 Restak, 18. *Cf.* Stassinopoulos, 38.
169 Restak, 18.
170 *ibid.*, 18.
171 Eibl-Eibesfeldt, 'Von der Kunst des Spielens', *Die Welt*, 158, quoted by Meves (1977b), 21.
172 *cf.* Meves (1977b), 22f. Christa Meves (1977a), 25–7, also tells of a family where the children were brought up in an emphatically non-gender-specific fashion, yet behaved in a definitely gender-specific way.

173 The position of Margaret Mead is partially given on the rear cover of Goldberg's book.
174 Goldberg, 29–34.
175 *ibid.*, 30, 199–207.
176 *ibid.*, 37ff.
177 Quoted in *ibid.*, 44. *Redbook* (October 1973), 48.
178 von Rad, 75.
179 Schedl, I, 122.
180 *cf.* the admittedly one-sided survey in Leist (1972), 13–47. As a corrective to the frequently overstated Christian hostility to the body, see the excellent book of Scharf.
181 Böhmerle, 3.
182 T. Culmann, *Die christliche Ethik*, Stuttgart, ²1874, 56, quoted by Höffner, 81.
183 This is shown very clearly in Böhmerle's conclusions:

> It is worth noting that the present kind of bodily differences between male and female somehow irritate the perception of every morally pure person, and that even more the present method of reproducing the human race is somewhat painful. This shows that what we have now is not the original, the divine (Böhmerle, 28f.).

184 von Rad, 60. *Cf.* Cassuto, 58.
185 Schwally, 171ff.
186 *cf.* Cassuto, 58.
187 *cf.* Plato, *Symposium*, 189d.
188 *cf.* Philo, *On Creation*, 184.
189 *cf.* Prümm, 552f.
190 *cf.* Höffner, 81.
191 *cf.* Kaltenbrunner, 19.
192 Ruppert, 39.
193 von Rad, 60. *Cf.* Procksch, 450.
194 Westermann, 145ff.
195 Wolff, 159.
196 Dillmann, 32.
197 Schedl, 221.
198 *ibid.*, 212.
199 *ibid.*
200 *cf.* Westermann, 155; Dillmann, 32; Strack, 3.
201 *cf.* Westermann, 149.
202 Dillmann, 32f.
203 Schedl, 222; *cf.* Westermann, 150; von Rad, 59; Hick, 49.
204 *cf.* Gössmann, 20f.
205 von Rad, 82.
206 Herder quoted by Westermann, 231.
207 Heinisch, 119. *Cf.* Reidick, 128.

208 Hick, 52. *Cf.* Ruppert, 54; Döller, 6.
209 Westermann, 232.
210 Zimmerli, 147. *Cf.* Procksch, 28.
211 Westermann, 232.
212 Dillmann, 66.
213 von Rad, 83.
214 Heinisch, 118.
215 von Rad, 84.
216 *ibid.*, 83.
217 Stein, 149f.
218 P. Brunner, 329.
219 Westermann, 262; *cf.* Walsh, 176f., 32.
220 Reidick, 26; *cf. ibid.*, 102: 'The role of helper, which Scripture ascribes to the woman, already entails her subordination.'
221 P. Brunner, 329ff.
222 Hick, 53.
223 Stein, 136. *Cf.* 1 Timothy 2:13!
224 According to P. Brunner, 330.
225 *ibid.*
226 *cf.* Walsh, 170, 176f.
227 Wenham (1978), 316.
228 Walsh, 170, 176.
229 Peter Brunner emphasises that 'the man's responsibility was greater than the woman's and therefore his guilt was really greater too' (Brunner, 330).
230 *ibid.* Brunner's quotation is not just based on Genesis 3, but also must be understood against the background of Romans 5:12 (*cf.* Hick, 192).
231 *cf.* Walsh, 165; König, 241; Heinisch, 121.
232 Stein, 151.
233 *e.g.*, Procksch, 31; Hetzenauer, 67; König, 261; Dillmann, 72; Heinisch, 120; von Rad, 90; Zerbst, 39; Hick, 192.
234 Heinisch, 120.
235 von Rad, 90.
236 Exodus 22:18 indicates that magic was associated with women in Old Testament times. This also seems to have been so in later Judaism, for Rabbi Hillel (died *c.* AD 20) coined the saying, 'The more women, the more witchcrafts' (m Aboth, 2:7).
237 According to Mauss, 62, among primitive peoples women are generally regarded as the 'real carriers' of magic (*cf. ibid.*, 152f. and Kampmann, II, 197). According to the anthropologist Schmidt, Shamanism, a magical-ecstatic practice among many primitive peoples, is developed by women and was originally practised only by women (Schmidt, 81). Another indication of women's greater openness to the occult is the strong tendency towards magical practices (witchcraft) in American feminism (*cf. Pardon* 7 (1979) 62f.).

238 *e.g.*, Heinisch, 128; von Rad, 93; Procksch, 37, *etc.*
239 Calvin, 172. Delitzsch, 166, says something similar: 'The subordination of the woman to the man was intended from the beginning; but now that the harmony of their mutual wills in God is destroyed, this subordination becomes subjection.'
240 Jacob, 118; Reidick, 102.
241 *cf.* Hick, 55; Reidick, 101.
242 Hick, 55
243 According to Thomas Aquinas, *Summa theologica*, Iq 92, art 1 ad 2, there already existed before the fall a kind of subordination of the woman (*subjectio oeconomica vel civilis*) which served the woman's 'advantage and well-being' (*ad . . . utilitatem et bonum*); *cf.* Nussbaumer, 145f.
244 According to Luther, Genesis 3:16 expresses 'natural law', which is not abolished by the gospel, but confirmed 'as God's created ordinance' (*WA* 50, 633, 22–4).
245 Jacob, 118; *cf.* Zerbst, 38.
246 Soggin, 930ff.
247 Westermann, 262.
248 *cf.* our interpretation of 1 Corinthians 14:34 on pp. 117–20.
249 *cf.* Wolff's translation, 170.
250 So Hick, 57.
251 *ibid.*
252 *ibid.*
253 We follow *ibid.*, 67, closely.
254 *cf.* Wolff, 179.
255 *cf.* Hick, 60.
256 Döller, 46; *cf.* Jenni, 33.
257 Jenni, 32ff.
258 *ibid.*, 34.
259 Wolff, 166.
260 *ibid.*, 167.
261 *ibid.*, 167.
262 *ibid.*, 167.
263 Hick, 63. *Cf.* Wolff, 168.
264 Hick, 64. *Cf.* Marquardt, 3.
265 Hick, 64.
266 Döller, 82.
267 On this interpretation of Genesis 1:27, and the devaluation of sexuality that goes with it, *cf.* pp. 59–63.
268 *cf.* Böhmerle, 28.
269 Wolff, 175.
270 Schniewind, 203.
271 Jeremias (1971), 212f.
272 Zimmermann, 122. *Cf.* Ketter, 367.

273 Ketter, 367. *Cf. Inter insigniores*, 20: 'This text [*i.e.*, Matt 22:30] does not mean . . . that the difference between male and female, so far as it determines personal identity, is abolished in glory.'

274 So Zimmermann, 128.

275 *ibid.*

276 It seems that wherever angels take human form in the Bible they appear to be male. The idea of female angels seems to be foreign to the Bible. Of course that does not mean we can conclude that there are no 'female' angels. We must leave open the possibility of their existence, as Holy Scripture does not give any detailed teaching about angels which would answer all the questions people have about them. But even if there are only 'male' angels, Matthew 22:30 cannot mean that the redeemed when perfect will become 'male', for the text does not speak of the blessed *becoming angels*, only that they will become *like* angels (*hōs angeloi*). In Matthew 18:3 Jesus says that only those who become *like* children (*hōs paidia*) will enter the kingdom of heaven. This example shows that the little word 'like' (*hōs*) does not denote complete identity, only similarity, for adults retain the characteristics of adulthood, even when they become like children in the sense of Matthew 18:3. Transferred to Matthew 22:30, that means that the redeemed retain their human character when they become 'like' the angels. This must at least allow for the possibility that they retain their sexual characteristics in their angelic existence. Peter Ketter has correctly pointed out that the expression 'like the angels' does not necessitate any abolition of sexuality. 'The creator's law "Increase and multiply" does not hold good in heaven. In *this* sense [my emphasis] man is like the angels there' (Ketter, 368).

277 *cf.* on Jesus' attitude to women, Ketter; Marquardt; Leipoldt, 79–98; Hick, 78–87; Belser, 327–38; Jeremias (1971), 223–7.

278 *cf.* on the position of women in Judaism at the time of Jesus, Leipoldt, 49–79; Hick, 69–77; Oepke, 781ff.

279 *Against Apion*, 2.201.

280 Strack-Billerbeck, III, 611.

281 Strack-Billerbeck, II, 495.

282 *cf.* Leipoldt, 56.

283 *cf. ibid.*, 66.

284 m Aboth 1.5 (Danby's translation).

285 *ibid.*

286 Jeremias (1969), 361.

287 Foerster, 127.

288 Leipoldt, 61.

289 *ibid.*, 75.

290 *ibid.*

291 Hick, 71.

292 *ibid.*

293 Quoted by Leipoldt, 71.
294 *cf. ibid.*, 71 and Hick, 71.
295 Strack-Billerbeck, III, 610; *cf.* the passages cited, 610f.
296 Kosmala, 230.
297 *ibid.*, 231.
298 According to Marquardt, 9.
299 *cf.* Belser, 335; Ketter, 274.
300 Hick, 84.
301 Weber, 16. *Cf.* Wenham (1984).
302 Esmein, 97f. *Cf.* Heth and Wenham.
303 Esmein, 97f.
304 The text does not say explicitly that it was women who brought their children to Jesus. But since Luke 18:15 describes them as babies, and the bringing up of small children was exclusively the work of women in those days, it may be surmised that the great majority were women, even if some fathers may have been present (*cf.* Ketter, 300ff.).
305 Though the identification of the 'disciple whom Jesus loved' (John 13:23; 19:26–7; 20:2–8; 21:7, 20–3) with the apostle John is rejected by the majority of exegetes, there are still good grounds for it; *cf.* Schlatter (1930b); Wikenhauser, 203–10; Bouyer (1968), 5–15; Robinson, 225–311; Morris, 215–80; Guthrie (1965), 213–39.
306 Gärtner, 9, emphasises this fact.
307 *ibid.*, 10.
308 *Inter insigniores*, 13.
309 Descamps, 50.
310 *cf.* pp. 73–5.
311 *cf.* Gärtner, 10f.
312 Hick, 82.
313 Beyer, 81f.
314 *cf.* Blum, 144.
315 *ibid.*
316 Ketter, 277.
317 Hick, 82.
318 Translation follows K. Haacker (1977b), 114f.
319 *ibid.*, 113–15.
320 Bornhäuser, 92.
321 The following discussion presupposes the authenticity of all the epistles ascribed to St Paul. Scholarship has sometimes raised some serious objections against the authenticity of the Pastoral Epistles (1 and 2 Timothy, Titus), Ephesians, Colossians and 2 Thessalonians, but these objections are not at all convincing. Our knowledge of the methods of composition of ancient letters (with secretaries often heavily influencing the content of letters) and of historical considerations permits the authenticity of all the Pauline letters to be maintained. *Cf.* Riesner, 5–7; Longenecker and Tenney, 281–97; Guthrie (1961), 92–246; Robinson, 31–85.

322 *e.g.*, Delling (1931), 62ff.
323 Paul is of course describing here the normal situation, so the passage may not be used against abstinence in old age or on health grounds.
324 *e.g.*, Delling (1931), 66–74.
325 Schlatter (1956), 219.
326 *ibid.*
327 *e.g.*, Moltmann-Wendel (1977), 22ff. and Ruether, 82f.
328 Ridderbos, 59.
329 *cf.*, on the women in the apostle's life, Haller, 14–46.
330 Michel, 381.
331 Haller, 44.
332 *cf.* Wikenhauser, 188f.; Haller, 20.
333 Schlier, 678.
334 *ibid.*
335 *cf.*, on the passages discussed, Cullmann, 311–14. To these should be added all the passages where Paul quotes an Old Testament passage about Yahweh and applies it to Christ (*e.g.*, Rom 10:11, 13, *etc.*).
336 W. Meyer (1945), 17.
337 *cf.* Schlatter (1956), 308: 'It is not referring to a veil which covers the face, but to a headscarf, as the comparison with the man's hairstyle makes plain.'
338 *Homily on 1 Corinthians*, 26. Homily III, quoted by Hick, 115.
339 Early church art shows women praying, with and without veils. *Cf.* Delling (1931), 97.
340 *cf.* Jaubert, 428.
341 *cf.* Schlatter (1956), 312.
342 Hooker, 413. *Cf.* Schlatter (1928), VI, 134: 'In approaching God the church presents herself before the heavenly spirits, who watch over God's order and take no pleasure in what destroys his creation. It is not good to pray so that the angels must, in disgust, avert their eyes from the one who prays.'
343 Jaubert, 422.
344 *cf.* also Hooker, 411; Isaksson, 175.
345 *cf.* Schlatter (1914), 23f.
346 *cf.* Bauer, 1485.
347 *cf. ibid.*, 915ff.
348 Schlatter (1928), VI, 180.
349 Kirschbaum, 50f.
350 Schlatter (1958), 89.
351 Schlatter (1936), 14.
352 Staab, 227.
353 Schlatter (1928), VIII, 143.
354 On this see our discussions on pp. 76–7.
355 Hick, 192.
356 Haller, 45.

357 Scholarship is divided whether Romans 16 is part of the original epistle, but there are good grounds for believing that it is original. *Cf.* Michel, 375f., 382.

358 Blum, 145; Michel, 377.

359 Paul describes Phoebe as 'a helper of many and of myself as well' (Rom 16:2).

360 Michel, 377. In the early church the duties of a deaconess included visiting, caring for the sick, and helping with the baptism of women. *Cf.* Leipoldt, 134f.

361 On the interpretation of this difficult verse, *cf.* Riesner, 52.

362 Karl Barth correctly recognises this when he writes that without the headship of the man, 'the man cannot be a man nor the woman a woman' (Barth, 84).

363 Tischleder, 124.

364 Ewald, 236.

365 Tischleder, 124. Ephesians 5:21 belongs grammatically with the preceding section, but it introduces the household code in 5:22–6:9.

366 Riesner, 51.

367 Delling (1969), 46.

368 *cf.* Häring, 1066.

369 Schlatter (1929), 399.

370 *cf.* Moltmann-Wendel (1977), 20; *Die Frau in Familie, Kirche und Gesellschaft*, 32.

371 Blass-Debrunner, 101.

372 *cf.* Sanday and Headlam, 422f.; Bauer, 751.

373 Schlatter (1928), IX, 47.

374 Schlatter (1937), 126.

375 von le Fort, 148.

376 Schlatter (1937), 128f.

377 Schlatter (1928), IX, 49.

378 *cf.* the definitely tendentious presentations in Leist (1972), 13–59 and Scharf, 109ff.

379 *cf.* Piper, 942.

380 Leist (1972), 20–3.

381 Quoted in Suppan, 41.

382 *ibid.*

383 *cf.* Piper, 942.

384 The following examples are taken from Scharf, 10ff.

385 *ibid.*, 10.

386 *cf.* Bailey, 62ff.; Müller, 56–65.

387 Quoted by Jelsma, 90.

388 So Lange, 141. Historians' estimates vary widely, from a few tens of thousands to a million (Jelsma, 94).

389 On the position of women before Christ, see Ketter, 3–57; Hick, 13–77.

390 Kahrstedt, 400.
391 Paulsen, 1346.
392 *cf.* Jelsma, 32.
393 *cf.* Leipoldt, 129f.
394 *cf. ibid.*, 130ff.
395 Leipoldt, 134f.; Frick, 922.
396 Leipoldt, 139.
397 Jelsma, 52.
398 *cf.* Beckwith, 37.
399 In 1970 seventy of the churches which belonged to the World Council of Churches favoured the ordination of women (Beckwith, 39). Among the Lutheran churches the Swedish church, under massive pressure from the state, first permitted it in 1958. In the German church the ordination of women is generally practised, except in Schaumburg-Lippi.
400 After the office of bishops had been in theory opened to women in many Protestant churches, the first consecration of a woman bishop in a major church took place in 1980, when the divorcee Marjorie Matthews was chosen as a bishop of the Methodist church of North America. The Episcopal Church of the USA followed suit in 1989 by consecrating Barbara Harris as Bishop of Massachusetts.
401 *cf.* Rengstorf (1953), 13f. Rengstorf refers to 1 Clement 1:3 (*c.* AD 95) and to Clement of Alexandria (about AD 200).
402 *cf.* Schlatter (1929), 398f.
403 *cf.* Barth, 94.
404 *cf.* E. Brunner, 395.
405 *cf.* Bonhoeffer, 43–7. Bonhoeffer (44) holds that setting aside the biblical ordering of the sexes has serious consequences: 'It is the beginning of the break-up, indeed the collapse, of all human organisation when the woman's supportive service is viewed as a lessening of or indeed an insult to her honour.'
406 Westermann, 232.
407 *cf.* Wenham (1978), 311.
408 Bouyer (1977), 13.
409 *cf.* pp. 152–62.
410 *cf.* Wenham (1978), 315f.
411 *cf.* Leipoldt, 17, 41–9; Hick, 36–46.
412 *cf.* Bouyer (1977), 12.
413 *ibid.* On female priests in the Greco-Roman world, see Hardy's essay. Also Oepke, 786f.
414 Rengstorf (1954), 25.
415 *cf.* Staab, 100; Rengstorf (1953), 135.
416 Quoted by E. Kähler, *Zeitschrift für evangelische Ethik* 3 (1959), 2f.
417 *cf.* E. Meyer, 256. The Roman *patria potestas* was, however, gradually curtailed in the imperial era, *cf.* Kahrstedt, 53.

418 *cf.* Rengstorf (1953), 134–6.
419 *cf.* pp. 49–51 above.
420 *cf. ibid.*
421 *cf.* Christenson (1971), 13, and the accounts of Morgan and Landorf's experiences.
422 This comes from the investigations of Farina and Dunhom, which we reproduce from Fuchs, Gaspari and Millendorfer, 157ff.
423 *cf.* Fuchs, Gaspari and Millendorfer, 160f., 163.
424 *cf.* Muldworf, 18, 27, 34f., 50, 89, 117–31.
425 *ibid.*, 142.
426 *ibid.*
427 *cf.* Fuchs, Gaspari and Millendorfer, 101f., 144, 179f.
428 *cf.* Huber, 77f.; Helbrügge, 59ff.; Hetzer, 1–8.
429 Hassenstein, 374.
430 Meves (1977a), 30.
431 Neumann, 103.
432 Muldworf, 30.
433 *cf.* Affemann, 65, 181–3; Bökmann, 100; Timmons, 12.
434 *cf.* Bodamer, 142.
435 *cf.* Bökmann, 98.
436 Bouyer (1977), 23f.
437 Lewis, 90f.
438 Jelsma, 150.
439 Röper, 84. *Cf. ibid.* '74 and Moltmann-Wendel (1979), 342.
440 *cf.* Lüthi, 195–7.
441 According to the feminist theologian Nelle Morton, divine titles such as 'Lord, King of the Universe, Almighty, Everlasting Father, Prince of Peace' are images expressing sovereignty and historical prejudice, whose one-sidedness must be overcome (*Die Frau in der Theologie*, 15).
442 H. David, 17.
443 Thomas Aquinas, *Summa Theologica*, Iq 93, art 4 ad 1. The Latin reads: *Nam vir est principium mulieris et finis sicut Deus est principium et finis totius creaturae.*
444 H. David, 14.
445 *cf.* our discussions on male spontaneity, which is the basis of marital union (p. 37–8) and which opens up the possibility of intellectual fatherhood (p. 45). For the Christian man there is the additional possibility of realising God's fatherhood and husbandhood in spiritual fatherhood 'in Christ' and spiritual husbandhood. On this, see the profound discussion of H. David, 28–50 (on spiritual fatherhood), and 51–72 (on spiritual husbandhood).
446 Quoted from Hertzka, 13.
447 Daly (1980), 5.
448 *ibid.*, 8.

449 *cf.* Schlatter (1928), VI, 113: 'Within nature no creature so constantly expresses what God is as the man does.'
450 *cf.* Bichlmeyer, 189: 'The man is the image of the creator, the woman image of the creation.'
451 The parallels Christ/husband and Church/wife in Ephesians 5:22ff. would be totally arbitrary and inappropriate if the man were not in a special sense an image of God (or Christ), and the woman in a special sense an image of the church (or creation)!
452 *e.g.*, Mayr, 250–5.
453 So Schrey, 232.
454 *cf.* the analysis of Schmidt-Kahler.
455 Höffner, 106.
456 Fuchs, Gaspari and Millendorfer, 157ff. The devastating consequences of the loss of fatherliness for sons and daughters is brilliantly described by Bodamer, 140ff.
457 *cf.* Müller-Schwefe, and Bodamer, 133–44.
458 J. David, 1239.
459 Bodamer, 140, correctly states that the modern man

> is no longer a father, because he no longer recognises a father above him. The concept of earthly father only survives because the father of all things, the original father, has delegated it to him the earthly father . . . Since the man today has himself become fatherless, he no longer has that higher legitimation; he is left to himself, and has no mirror in which to see himself and to correct him.

460 Berdyaev quoted by Elliot, 158.
461 Erler, 9.
462 Meves (1977a), 29. *Cf.* E. Brunner, 361: 'The test of a truly emancipatory movement must always be that the differences between the sexes are not abolished, but set out correctly in their purity.'
463 Quoted by Kampmann, I, 91.
464 *cf.* pp. 149–51.
465 *e.g.*, the books of Stein, von le Fort, Schneider, Firkel, Arnold, Kampmann, Bouyer. Protestant books include Trobisch, Elliot, Evans-Weiss.
466 On this see the important analysis of Bockmühl.
467 Among honourable exceptions are the presentations of Mary by Schlatter (1930a), Asmussen, W. Arnold and Lamparter. *Cf.* also the beautiful essay by W. Meyer (1959).
468 Schlatter (1929), 398.
469 Quoted by Nigg, 69.
470 See the description of Luther's position in Brunotte, 193–9, and in P. Brunner, 313–15.
471 Ziegler, 232–69, has shown in a detailed analysis that because of his sex-related characteristics the man is specially equipped for leadership.

Conversely the man 'is less good at obeying, the woman less good at giving orders' (265).

472 Schlatter (1929), 129.

473 Dora Rappard, whose preaching ministry has brought great blessing to many women, has urged with great seriousness that evangelistic preaching by women in no way imperils the man's teaching office. 'A Christian woman may not take on a real teaching ministry within the church . . . One must not be deceived by momentary success! The holy ordinances cannot be set aside without damage' (quoted by Veiel-Rappard, 205).

474 H. David, 46f.

475 Daly (1986), 96.

Bibliography

R. Affemann, *Sexualität im Leben junger Menschen*, Freiburg, 1978.

F. X. Arnold, *Die Frau in der Kirche*, Nürnberg, 1949.

W. Arnold, *Maria, die Mutter Jesu Christi*, Witten, 1971.

F. v. Baader, *Sämtliche Werke*, Leipzig, 1850.

D. S. Bailey, *The Man-Woman Relation in Christian Thought*, London, 1959.

K. Barth, *Mann und Frau*, München and Hamburg, 1964.

W. Bauer, *Griechisch-Deutsches Wörterbuch zu den Schriften des Neuen Testaments und der übrigen christlichen Literatur*, Berlin and New York, 1971.

E. Baulieu and F. Haeur, 'Die physiologischen und pathologischen Unterschiede zwischen Mann und Frau', in Sullerot, pp. 155–85.

S. de Beauvoir, *The Second Sex*, London, 1953.

R. T. Beckwith, 'The Office of Women in the Church to the Present Day', in Bruce and Duffield, pp. 26–39.

J. E. Belser, 'Die Frau in den neutestamentlichen Schriften', *Theologische Quartalschrift*, 1909, pp. 321–51.

W. Beyer, 'Diakoneo', in *Theological Dictionary of the New Testament* vol. 2, pp. 81–93.

G. Bichlmeyer, *Der Mann Jesus*, Wien, 1948.

F. Blass and A. Debrunner, *Grammatik des neutestamentlichen Griechisch*, Göttingen, 1976.

G. G. Blum, 'Das Amt der Frau im Neuen Testament', *Novum Testamentum* 7 (1965), pp. 142–61.

K. Bockmühl, *Atheismus in der Christenheit. Anfechtung und Überwindung. Erster Teil: Die Unwirklichkeit Gottes in Theologie und Kirche*, Wuppertal, 1969.

J. Bodamer, *Der Mann von heute. Seine Gestalt und Psychologie*, Freiburg und München, 1965.

T. Böhmerle, *Die Frauenfrage im Lichte der Bibel*, Reutlingen, 1951.

J. Bökmann, 'Verhaltensbiologie und Ethik', *Theologie der Gegenwart* 19 (1977), pp. 97–101.

D. Bonhoeffer, *Widerstand und Ergebung*, München, 1955.

K. Bornhäuser, *Die Bergpredigt*, Gütersloh, [2]1927.

L. Bouyer, *Das vierte Evangelium*, Salzburg, 1968.

idem, *Frau und Kirche*, Einsiedeln, 1977.

M. Bruce and G. E. Duffield (ed.), *Why Not? Priesthood and Ministry of Women. Revised and augmented Edition. Prepared by R. T. Beckwith*, 1976.

E. Brunner, *Das Gebot und die Ordnungen. Entwurf einer protestantisch-theologischen Ethik*, New York, o.J. (=1932).

P. Brunner, 'Das Hirtenamt und die Frau', in *Pro Ecclesia, Gesammelte Aufsätze zur systematischen Theologie*, Berlin und Hamburg, 1962, pp. 310–38.

W. Brunotte, *Das geistliche Amt bei Luther*, Berlin, 1959.

F. J. J. Buytendijk, *Die Frau. Natur, Erscheinung, Dasein*, Köln, 1953.

J. Calvin, *A Commentary on Genesis*, London, 1847.

U. Cassuto, *A Commentary on the book of Genesis*, vol. 1, Jerusalem, 1961.

L. Christenson, *The Christian Family*, London, 1971.

L. and N. Christenson, *Das christliche Ehepaar*, Erzhausen, 1978.

M. Clara, *Die Bestimmung des Geschlechtes beim Menschen*, Leipzig, 1943.

S. B. Clark, *Man and Woman in Christ*, Ann Arbor, 1980.

O. Cullmann, *The Christology of the New Testament*, London, [2]1963.

R. Dahrendorf, *Homo Sociologicus*, London, 1973.

M. Daly, *Beyond God the Father*, London, 1986.

idem, *Jenseits von Gottvater, Sohn & Co*, Munich, 1980.

H. David, *Über das Bild des christlichen Mannes*, Freiburg, 1953.

J. David, 'Vater', in *Katholisches Soziallexikon*, ed. A. Klose, Innsbruck, 1964, cc. 1239–41.

F. Delitzsch, *New Commentary on Genesis*, vol. 1, Edinburgh, 1888.

G. Delling, *Paulus' Stellung zu Frau und Ehe*, Stuttgart, 1931.

idem, 'Hypotasso', in *Theological Dictionary of the New Testament*, vol. 8, 1969, pp. 40–2.

A. Descamps, 'Welche Bedeutung hat die Haltung Christi und die

Praxis der Apostel für uns heute?' in *Die Sendung der Frau in der Kirche*, pp. 48–53.

A. Dillmann, *Die Genesis*, Leipzig, [6]1892.

J. Döller, *Das Weib im Alten Testament*, Münster in Westfalen, 1920.

E. F. W. Eberhard, *Feminismus und Kulturuntergang. Die erotischen Grundlagen der Frauenemanzipation*, Wien und Leipzig, [2]1927.

L. Eckstein, *Die Sprache der menschlichen Leibeserscheinung*, Leipzig, 1943.

E. Elliot, *Let me be a Woman*, London, 1979.

U. Erler, *Zerstörung und Selbstzerstörung der Frau, Emanzipationskampf der Geschlechter auf Kosten des Kindes*, Stuttgart, 1977.

A. Esmein, *Le mariage en droit canonique*, I, Paris, [2]1905.

Evangelisches Kirchenlexikon (abbr. *EKL*), ed., H. Brunotte und O. Weber, I, Göttingen, [2]1961, II und III, Göttingen, [2]1962.

U. Evans-Weiss, *Frau sein – frei sein. Von der Emanzipation zur Freiheit*, Wuppertal, 1979.

P. Ewald, *Die Briefe des Paulus an die Epheser, Kolosser und Philemon*, Leipzig, 1905.

H. J. Eysenck, *The Inequality of Man*, London, 1973.

S. Firestone, *The Dialectic of Sex: The Case for Feminist Revolution*, London, 1971.

E. Firkel, *Die Bedeutung der Frau in unserer Zeit*, Düsseldorf, 1956.

W. Foerster, *Palestinian Judaism in New Testament Times*, Edinburgh, 1964.

G. v. le Fort, *Die ewige Frau, Die Frau in der Zeit. Die zeitlose Frau*, München, 1934.

Die Frau in Familie, Kirche und Gesellschaft, Eine Studie zum gemeinsamen Leben von Frau und Mann. Vorgelegt von einem Ausschuss der Evangelischen Kirche in Deutschland, Gütersloh, 1979.

Die Frau in der Theologie. Dokumentation, Ev. Pressedienst (epd) Nr. 44 (1976).

J. Freundorfer, 'Die Pastoralbriefe', in *Regensburger Neues Testament*, vol. 7, Paulusbriefe II, Regensburg, [3]1959, pp. 201–308.

R. Frick, 'Weibliche Diakonie', *EKL*, I, cc. 921–6.

A. Fuchs, C. Gaspari and J. Millendorfer, *Makropsychologische Untersuchung der Familie in Europa*, Wien, 1977.

B. Gärtner, 'Das Amt, der Mann und die Frau im Neuen Testament', in *signo crucis*, 1963, pp. 7–24.

S. Goldberg, *The Inevitability of Patriarchy*, London, 1977.

E. Gössmann, *Mann und Frau in Familie und Öffentlichkeit*, München, 1964.

D. Guthrie, *New Testament Introduction, The Pauline Epistles*, London, 1961; *The Gospel and Acts*, 1965.

K. Haacker (a), 'Emanzipation der Frau – eine Konsequenz des Evangeliums?', *Porta* 23 (1977), pp. 9–24.

idem (b), 'Der Rechtssatz Jesu zum Thema Ehebruch (Mt 5, 28)', *Biblische Zeitschrift*, 1 (1977), pp. 113–16.

J. Haller, *Die Frauen des apostolischen Zeitalters*, Stuttgart, 1936.

E. R. Hardy, 'The Priestess in the Greco-Roman World', in Bruce and Duffield, pp. 26–39.

B. Häring, *Das Gesetz Christi. Moraltheologie*, Freiburg, [3]1954.

B. Hassenstein, *Verhaltensbiologie des Kindes*, München, 1978.

M. Hauke, *Women in the Priesthood? A Systematic Analysis in the Light of the Order of Creation and Redemption*, Dublin, 1988.

P. Heinisch, *Das Buch Genesis*, Bonn, 1930.

W. Heitler, *Die Natur und das Göttliche*, Zug, 1974.

T. Hellbrügge (ed.), *Probleme des behinderten Kindes*, München-Berlin-Wien, 1973, pp. 59–80.

G. Hertzka, *So heilt Gott, Die Medizin der Heiligen Hildegard*, Stein am Rhein, [6]1978.

W. A. Heth and G. J. Wenham, *Jesus and Divorce*, London, 1984.

M. Hetzenauer, *Commentarius in Librum Genesis*, Graz-Wien, 1910.

H. Hetzer, *Mütterlichkeit. Psychologische Untersuchung der Grundformen mütterlicher Haltung*, Leipzig, 1937.

L. Hick, *Stellung des heiligen Paulus zur Frau im Rahmen seiner Zeit*, Köln, 1957.

J. Höffner, *Christliche Gesellschaftslehre*, Kevelaer, [6]1975.

P. Hofstätter, *Psychologie, Das Fischer Lexicon*, Frankfurt a.M., 1962.

G. Höhler, 'Kommt das Heil von den Frauen? Frauenbewegung heute, Gefahren und Möglichkeiten', *Die Politische Meinung* 173 (1977), pp. 13–24.

M. D. Hooker, 'Authority on her Head: An Examination of 1 Cor. XI.10', *New Testament Studies* 10 (1974), pp. 410–16.

R. Huber, 'Emanzipation oder Feminismus? Biologische Überlegungen zur Mann-Frau-Beziehung', in Kaltenbrunner, pp. 50–84.

C. Hutt, *Males and Females*, Penguin Science of Behaviour, 1972.

'Inter insigniores, Erklärung der Kongregation für die Glaubenslehre zur Frage der Zulassung der Frauen zum Priesteramt', in *Die Sendung der Frau in der Kirche*, pp. 11–25.

A. Isaksson, *Marriage and Ministry in the New Temple*, Lund, 1965.

B. Jacob, *Das erste Buch der Tora – Genesis*, Berlin, 1934.

F. Janowski, 'Amerikanische Frauenliteratur', *Evangelische Kommentare* 6 (1979), pp. 347–9.

A. Jaubert, 'Le voile des femmes (1. Cor, XI.2–16)', *New Testament Studies* 18 (1972), pp. 419–30.

A. J. Jelsma, *Heilige und Hexen. Die Stellung der Frau im Christentum*, Konstanz, 1977.

E. Jenni, 'Adon, Herr', in *Theologisches Handwörterbuch zum Alten Testament*, ed. E. Jenni and C. Westermann, vol. I, München-Zürich, 1971, pp. 31–8.

J. Jeremias, *Jerusalem in the Time of Jesus*, London, 1969.

idem, New Testament Theology, vol. I: The Proclamation of Jesus, London, 1971.

S. Kahl, H. Langer, H. Leistner, E. Moltmann-Wendel, *Feministische Theologie-Praxis. Ein Werkstattbuch*, Bad Boll, 1981.

U. Kahrstedt, *Kulturgeschichte der römischen Kaiserzeit*, Bern, 1958.

G. K. Kaltenbrunner (ed.), *Verweiblichung als Schicksal? Verwirrung im Rollenspiel der Geschlechter*, München, 1978.

T. Kampmann, *Die Methodologie der Geschlechterdifferenz und die Physiologie des Frauenwesens* (2 volumes), Paderborn, 1946.

P. Ketter, *Christ and Womankind*, London, 1937.

C. v. Kirschbaum, *Die wirkliche Frau*, Zollikon-Zürich, 1949.

E. König, *Die Genesis*, Gütersloh, ³1925.

H. Kosmala, 'Von der Stellung der Frau im Judentum', *Judaica* 4 (1948), pp. 225–32.

E. v. Kuehneldt-Leddihn, *Das Rätsel Liebe. Leidenschaft, Lust, Leid und Laster. Materialien für eine Geschlechtertheologie*, Wien-München, 1975.

idem, 'Wider den Rollentausch der Geschlechter. Die Frau im Katholischen Glauben', *Die Politische Meinung* 173 (1977), pp. 35–45.

K. v. Kühlwetter, 'Frauenbewegung', in *EKL*, I, pp. 1358–62.

W. Kuhn, *Biologischer Materialismus. Der Mensch ist keine Machine*, Osnabrück, 1973.

H. Lamparter, *Die Magd des Herrn. Ein evangelisches Marienbild*, Metzingen, 1979.

J. Landorf, *Stark und zart. Wie sich eine Frau den Mann wünscht*, Marburg, 1977.

E. Lange, 'Hexenglaube', in *EKL*, II, pp. 140f.

J. Leipoldt, *Die Frau in der antiken Welt und im Urchristentum*, Gütersloh, 1962.

F. Leist, *Liebe und Geschlecht*, Freiburg, 1970.

idem, *Der sexuelle Notstand und die Kirchen*, Gütersloh, [2]1972.

P. Lersch, *Vom Wesen der Geschlechter*, München-Basel, [4]1968.

C. S. Lewis, 'Priestesses in the Church?', in *God in the Dock*, London, 1979, pp. 87–94.

H. Lietzmann, *An die Römer*, Tübingen, [3]1971.

R. N. Longenecker and M. C. Tenney, *New Dimensions in New Testament Study*, Grand Rapids, 1974.

I. Lück, *Alarm um die Schule, Kritische Auseinandersetzung mit der gegenwärtigen Erziehungs-Situation. Die Neomarxistische Unterwanderung*, Stuttgart, 1979.

M. Luther, 'Von den Konziliis und Kirchen', in *Kritische Gesamtausgabe*, Weimar, 1914 (abgekurzt WA), vol. 50, pp. 488–653.

K. Lüthi, *Gottes neue Eva: Wandlungen des Weiblichen*, Stuttgart, 1978.

G. Marquardt, 'Die Stellung der Frau in den Evangelien', *Bibel und Kirche* 11 (1956), pp. 2–10.

M. Mauss, *Soziologie und Anthropologie, Vol. 1, Theologie und Magie. Soziale Morphologie*, München, 1974.

F. K. Mayr, 'Patriarchalisches Gottesverständnis? Historische Erwägungen zur Trinitätslehre, *Theologische Quartalschrift* 152 (1972), pp. 224–55.

M. Mead, *Male and Female*, London, 1949.

J. Menschick (ed.), *Grundlagentexte zur Frauenemanzipation*, Köln, [2]1977.

E. Metzke, 'Anthropologie der Geschlechter, Philosophische Bemerkungen zum Stand der Diskussion', *Theologische Rundschau*, 22 (1954), pp. 211–41.

C. Meves (a), 'Missverständnis Emanzipation', in *Die Politische Meinung* 173 (1977), pp. 25–34.

idem (b), 'Der Hass auf den Unterschied – sind Männer und Frauen verschieden?', *Chancen und Krisen der modernen Ehe*, Kassel, 1977, pp. 13–30.

E. Meyer, *Römischer Staat und Staatsgedanke*, Zürich-München, [4]1975.

W. Meyer, *Der erste Brief an die Korinther*, 2nd Part, Zürich, 1945.

idem, 'Maria als Bild der Gnade und Heiligkeit', in M. Roesle und O. Cullmann (ed.), *Begegnung der Christen. Studien evangelischer und katholischer Theologen*, Stuttgart und Frankfurt a.M., 1959.

O. Michel, *Der Brief an die Römer*, Göttingen, [4]1966.

P. J. Möbius, *Ueber den physiologischen Schwachsinn des Weibes*, Halle a.d.S., [9]1908.

E. Moltmann-Wendel, *Freiheit, Gleichheit, Schwesterlichkeit. Zur Emanzipation der Frau in Kirche und Gesellschaft*, München, 1977.

idem, 'Feministische Theologie', *Evangelische Kommentare* 6 (1979), pp. 340–47.

M. Morgan, *Die totale Frau*, Zürich, 1978.

L. Morris, *Studies in the Fourth Gospel*, Grand Rapids, 1969.

B. Muldworf, *Von Beruf Vater*, Zürich-Köln, 1975.

M. Müller, *Grundlagen der katholischen Sexualethik*, Regensburg, 1968.

H. R. Müller-Schwefe, *Die Welt ohne Väter, Gedanken eines Christen zur Krise der Autorität*, Hamburg, 1957.

G. H. Neumann, 'Über den Umgang mit Säuglingen aus verhaltensbiologischer Sicht', *Theologie der Gegenwart* 19 (1977), pp. 101–4.

W. Nigg, *Niklaus von Flüe. In Berichten von Zeitgenossen*, Olten und Freiburg, 1980.

A. Nussbaumer, 'Der hl. Thomas und die rechtliche Stellung der Frau. Eine Abwehr und Richtigstellung', in *Divus Thomas, Jahrbuch für Philosophie und spekulative Theologie* (1933), pp. 63–75 and 138–56.

W. Oddie, *What Will Happen to God? Feminism and the Reconstruction of Christian Belief*, London, 1984.

A. Oepke, 'Gynē', in *Theological Dictionary of the New Testament*, vol. I, pp. 776–90.

M. Offenberg, 'Frauenbewegung', *Lexikon für Theologie und Kirche*, vol. IV, Freiburg, 1960, pp. 303–5.

A. Paulsen, 'Frau', *EKL*, I, cc. 1344–9.

O. A. Piper, 'Sexualethik', *EKL*, III, cc. 941–4.

A. Portmann, *Biologische Fragmente zu einer Lehre vom Menschen*, Basel-Stuttgart, [3]1949.

O. Procksch, *Die Genesis*, Leipzig, [3]1924.

K. Prümm, *Religionsgeschichtliches Handbuch für den Raum der altchristlichen Umwelt*, Rom, 1954.

G. von Rad, *Genesis*, London, [2]1972.

G. Reidick, *Die hierarchische Struktur der Ehe*, München, 1953.

K. H. Rengstorf, 'Die neutestamentlichen Mahnungen an die Frau, sich dem Manne unterzuordnen', *Verbum Dei manet in Aeternum, Festschrift für O. Schmitz*, 1953.

idem, Mann und Frau im Christentum, Köln-Opladen, 1954.

R. M. Restak, 'Frauen denken wirklich anders', *Das Beste aus Reader's Digest*, I (1980), pp. 17–21.

H. N. Ridderbos, *Paul. An Outline of his Theology*, London, 1977.

R. Riesner, *Apostolischer Gemeindebau. Die Herausforderung der paulinischen Gemeinden*, Giessen-Basel, 1978.

P. Riessler, *Altjüdisches Schrifttum ausserhalb der Bibel*, Heidelberg, [2]1966.

J. A. T. Robinson, *Redating the New Testament*, London, 1976.

A. Röper, *Ist Gott ein Mann? Ein Gespräch mit Karl Rahner*, Düsseldorf, 1979.

J. Rötzer, *Menschenbild, Sexualität und Ehe, Grundriss einer evolutiven Anthropologie*, Frankfurt a.M., 1969.

R. Rüegg, *Ehe und Gemeinde*, Schiers, [5]1976.

R. R. Ruether, *Frauen für eine neue Gesellschaft, Frauenbewegung und menschliche Befreiung*, München, 1979.

L. Ruppert, *Das Buch Genesis*, Düsseldorf, 1976.

L. M. Russell, *The Liberating Word: A Guide to Non-Sexist Interpretation of the Bible*, Philadelphia, 1976.

W. Sanday and A. C. Headlam, *The Epistle to the Romans*, London, 1958.

G. Scharf, *Sexualität einst und heute. Fakten. Normen, Antworten*, Münster, 1978.

C. Schedl, *Geschichte des Alten Testaments, 1. Bd., Alter Orient und Urgeschichte*, Innsbruck-Wien-München, [2]1964.

M. Scheler, *Das Fiasko. Die herrenlose Frau*, Zürich, 1974.

A. Schlatter, 'Die korinthische Theologie', in *Beiträge zur Förderung christlicher Theologie* (1914).

idem, Die Korintherbriefe, Schlatters Erläuterungen zum Neuen Testament, 6. Teil, Stuttgart, 1928.

idem, Die Briefe an die Thessalonicher, Philipper, Timotheus und Titus, Schlatters Erläuterungen zum Neuen Testament, 8. Teil, Stuttgart, 1928.

idem, Die Briefe des Petrus, Judas, Jakobus, der Brief an die Hebräer, Schlatters Erläuterungen zum Neuen Testament, 9. Teil, Stuttgart, [5]1928.

idem, Die christliche Ethik, Stuttgart, ³1929.

idem (a), *Marienreden*, Velbert, ²1930.

idem (b), *Der Evangelist Johannes*, Stuttgart, 1930.

idem, Was sagt das Neue Testament der Frau?, Berlin-Dahlem, ²1936.

idem, Petrus und Paulus, Nach dem ersten Petrusbrief, Stuttgart, 1937.

idem, Paulus, der Bote Jesu, Eine Deutung seiner Briefe an die Korinther, Stuttgart, ²1956.

idem, Die Kirche der Griechen im Urteil des Paulus. Eine Auslegung seiner Briefe an Timotheus und Titus, Stuttgart, 1958.

H. Schlier, 'Kephalē' in *Theological Dictionary of the New Testament*, vol. III, pp. 672–81.

W. Schmidt, 'Leben und Wirken ältester Menschheit', in A. Randa (ed.), *Handbuch der Weltgeschichte*, Olten-Freiburg i.B., ³1962, cc. 59–90.

G. Schmidtchen, 'Auskunft über Frauen, Geschlechtsrollendifferenzierung soziologisch betrachtet', in Weinzierl, pp. 9–42.

T. Schmidt-Kahler, 'Kurskorrektur tut Not. Ursachen und Folgen der Bevölkerungsentwicklung', in *Die Politische Meinung* 1975 (1977), pp. 29–38.

O. Schneider, *Die Macht der Frau*, Salzburg-Leipzig, ⁵1938.

J. Schniewind, *Das Evangelium nach Matthäus*, Göttingen, 1968.

H. H. Schrey, 'Ist Gott ein Mann? Zur Forderung einer feministischen Theologie', *Theologische Rundschau*, 3 (1979), pp. 227–38.

F. Schwally, 'Die biblischen Schöpfungsberichte', in *Archiv für Religionswissenschaft*, ed. A. Dietrich, vol. 9 (1906), pp. 159–75.

A. Schwarzer, *Der kleine Unterschied und seine grossen Folgen*, Frankfurt a.M., 1975.

W. Siebel (ed.), *Herrschaft und Liebe, Zur Soziologie der Familie*, Berlin, 1984.

J. A. Soggin, 'msl herrschen', *Theologisches Handwörterbuch zum Alten Testament*, vol. I, 930–3.

K. Staab, 'Die Thessalonicherbriefe. Die Gefangenschaftsbriefe', in *Regensburger Neues Testament*, 7. Bd. *Paulusbriefe II*, Regensburg, ³1959, pp. 5–200.

A. A. Stassinopoulos, *The Female Woman*, London, 1973.

E. Stein, *Die Frau in Ehe und Beruf. Bildungsfragen heute*, Freiburg, 1963.

W. Stern, *Psychologie der frühen Kindheit bis zum sechsten Lebensjahre*, Leipzig, [4]1927.

A. Stopczyk, *Was Philosophen über Frauen denken*, München, 1980.

H. Strack, *Genesis, Exodus, Leviticus und Numeri*, München, 1893.

H. L. Strack and P. Billerbeck, *Kommentar zum Neuen Testament aus Talmud und Midrasch*, vol. II and III, München, [5]1969.

E. Sullerot, *Die Wirklichkeit der Frau*, München, 1979.

K. Suppan, *Die Ehelehre Martin Luthers, Theologische und rechtshistorische Aspekte des reformatorischen Eheverständnisses*, Salzburg-München, 1971.

L. Swidler, 'Jesus was a Feminist', *Catholic World* 212 (1970/71), pp. 177–83.

Thomas von Aquin, *Vollständige, ungekürzte deutsch-lateinische Ausgabe der Summa Theologica*, vol. 7, München-Heidelberg, 1941.

L. Tiger, *Warum die Männer wirklich herrschen. Die provozierende Antwort auf Klischees der Emanzipation*, München, 1973.

T. Timmons, *Ehe nach Gottes Plan*, Stuttgart, [2]1977.

P. Tischleder, *Wesen und Stellung der Frau nach der Lehre des heiligen Paulus*, Münster, 1923.

C. Tresmontant, *Biblisches Denken und hellenistische Überlieferung*, Düsseldorf, 1956.

I. Trobisch, *Mit Freuden Frau sein und was der Mann dazu tun kann*, Wuppertal, 1974.

E. Veiel-Rappard, *Mutter, Bilder aus dem Leben von Dorah Rappard-Gobat*, Giessen-Basel, [4]1929.

J. T. Walsh, 'Genesis 2, 46–3, 24. A Synchronic Approach', *Journal of Biblical Literature* 96 (1977), pp. 161–77.

M. Weber, *Die Idee der Ehe und die Ehescheidung*, Frankfurt, 1929.

O. Weininger, *Geschlecht und Charakter. Eine prinzipielle Untersuchung*, Wien, [28]1928.

E. Weinzierl (ed.), *Emanzipation der Frau. Zwischen Biologie und Ideologie*, Düsseldorf, 1980.

G. J. Wenham, 'The Ordination of Women: Why is it so divisive?' in *The Churchman* 92 (1978), pp. 310–19.

idem, 'Gospel Definitions of Adultery and Women's Rights', *Expository Times* 95 (1984), pp. 330–2.

C. Westermann, *Genesis 1–11*, Minneapolis, 1984.

A. Wikenhauser, *Einleitung in das Neue Testament*, Freiburg, [2]1956.

S. F. Witelson, 'Geschlechtsspezifische Unterschiede in der Neurologie der kognitiven Funktion und ihre psychologischen, sozialen, edukativen und klinischen Implikationen', in Sullerot, pp. 341–68.

H. W. Wolff, *The Anthropology of the Old Testament*, London, 1974.

J. Zander, 'Das Andere in unserem Geschlecht. Zur Verschiedenheit der Geschlechter aus der Sicht eines Arztes', in Weinzierl, pp. 57–66.

R. Zazzo, 'Einige Bemerkungen über die Unterschiede in der Psychologie der Geschlechter', in Sullerot, pp. 311–21.

E. Zerbst, *Das Amt der Frau in der Kirche. Eine praktisch-theologische Untersuchung*, Wien o.J.

A. Ziegler, *Das natürliche Entscheidungsrecht des Mannes in Ehe und Familie. Ein Beitrag zur Frage der Gleichberechtigung von Mann und Frau*, Heidelberg-Löwen, 1958.

W. Zimmerli, *1. Mose 1–11. Die Urgeschichte*, Zürich, [3]1967.

F. Zimmermann, *Die beiden Geschlechter in der Absicht Gottes. Zur Metaphysik der Geschlechter*, Wiesbaden, 1936.

Scriptural Index

Figures in bold denote chapter numbers, and figures in italics, verse numbers.

Index

Abba appellation, 155
abortion, 16, 18
Abraham, 171; daughter of, 96
abstract thought, 42–3, 49, 147
active and passive, 36–7, 48, 100–1, 157–8, 161
Adam, *see*: creation story; fall
adam, 66
adaptability, 34–5, 38, 48, 147
adolescence, 151, 165
adon, 85–6
adultery, Hebrew law on, 87
affirmation of sexuality, 180: Christian art, 136; church tradition, 135–6; New Testament, 88–92, 102–7, 130, 134, 175; Old Testament, 60–3, 81–3
agapē, 146
ama, 86
ancient world, 83, 135, 144, 145–6, 173; *see also*: philosophy; Judaism
androgynous creation, 61–3, 88–89
angels, 90, 91, 92, 114, 115
animal: devaluation of sex as, 27, 61; superiority of humans over, 64, 65, 71, 73, 75, 147
Annunciation, 78
anthropology, 52–3, 55, 78
antisomatism, clerical, 135–6
apostles: Jesus choice of male 98–9,

114, 144, 152, 153, 173; Junia, 131–2
Aquila (friend of Paul), 110, 132
arranging; aptitude, 33, 34, 49–50
art, 51, 136
asceticism, 102, 135–6; *see also* celibacy
attitudes of sexes to each other, 73–8
Augustine of Hippo, 91, 135, 178
authority: of Bible, 11, 12, 21, 56, 140, 168; *exousia*, 114–15; hierarchy in creation, 74–7, 78, 111, 115–16, 118–21, 122; rejection of, 165, 171–2; *see also*: responsibility; validity

Baader, Franz von, 32, 63
ba'al, 85–6
Babylonian law, 83
baptism, 136
Barth, Karl, 143, 195
Beauvoir, Simone de, 16–17
behaviour, study of, 55, 56, 151
Berdyaev, Nicholas, 63
Bible: authority, 11, 12, 21, 56, 140, 168; own interpreter, 81; non-sexist translation, 20; *see also*: New Testament; Old Testament; *and under* conditioning
Biblical Feminists, 20
blood, constitution of, 40

215